PRAISE

Seth's always present po[...] [...] an inspiration to all of us! His perseverance and resiliency is something I hope to emulate in my life. Our team has been privileged to know Seth and for that I thank you.

Bharat Guthikonda, MD, FACS, FAANS
Chairman of the Department of Neurosurgery at LSU Health, Shreveport;
Chair of the Medico-Legal Committee of the Council of State Neurosurgical
Societies; Member of the Executive Committee of the Council of State
Neurosurgical Societies; Diplomate of the American Board of Neurological Surgery

For me, being around Seth on a personal level as well as seeing him test, train, and compete was awesome. I got to see his drive to keep pushing forward no matter what was going on in his life in addition to witnessing his selflessness and love for others. Every time I see him, he gives me a big hug and tells me that "I pray for you" and "Love you." That is wonderful to experience because it is genuine.

I talk about him every quarter in my undergraduate exercise physiology course to let students know what happened to him as well as make them aware of what a person can accomplish with the desire to push through it while having loved ones surrounding them. I know it makes an impact on the students' lives because they have never heard a story quite like Seth's. He is a one-of-a-kind person that is always happy and laughing. He and Kimber want to share his story to inspire others to overcome whatever obstacles or challenges they may have in front of them. Reading this book will accomplish that goal.

David J. Szymanski, PhD, CSCS, D, RSCC*E, FNSCA
Department Chair & Professor, Director of Baseball Performance
Eva Cunningham Endowed Professorship in Education
PowerLift Sport Science Educational Board Member
Department of Kinesiology, Louisiana Tech University

This book, Push through it, is a game changer. Kimber did an awesome job reminding us how our words frame our lives. As I was reading this book, the thought came to me that this book is a warfare manual. This book is a mind-shifter. A Faith activator. A crushed heart mender. This book changed my life. I feel like I can move mountains. I know I can do all things through Christ who strengthens me. Throughout this book, I was so encouraged at the testimonies and life-giving examples. Kimber is walking us into our freedom chapter by chapter.

PUSH THROUGH IT is a book that everyone needs to have in their library as a go-to book whenever you feel weary, defeated, or hopeless. Kimber so beautifully paints us a picture of seasons in her life where she literally had to Trust God. She shows us how to reroute our thoughts on a good God.

I believe as you read "Push Through it" you are going to see mountains moved, devastation turned to destiny. Your scars turned into stars. This book is going to set your gaze towards heaven and you will see the victory. I feel it!

Pastor Kimberly Jones (known as Real Talk Kim)
Senior Pastor at Limitless Church in Fayetteville, GA

Seth's story is one of inspiration and unwavering faith. His story made me realize just how important our faith is, and how a little faith, mixed with a whole lot of determination can be life-changing. The greatest impact of the story was how Seth looked beyond the pain and devastation of his tragic accident and found it in his heart to forgive. The moment he chose to forgive the women who hit him showed me how big Seth's heart is and how much he loves God. This book will change your life, and cause you to want to love more, forgive daily, and live life like every day could be your last.

Dr. Kennita L. Williams, DDiv, DTh
Clear Vision Ministries

PUSH THROUGH IT!

PUSH THROUGH IT!

THE SETH HANCHEY STORY

HOW TO FIND
PURPOSE
IN YOUR PAIN

KIMBER HANCHEY-OGDEN

To request permissions, contact the publisher at KimberHancheyOgden@gmail.com.

Typesetting and Design by David W. Edelstein

ISBN:
Paperback: 979-8-9871075-0-8
Ebook: 979-8-9871075-1-5
Audiobook: 979-8-9871075-2-2

To my son, Seth, there would be no story without you.
Everyone needs a hero, and you are mine.
You are my daily dose of inspiration, always reminding
me to look up and keep my eyes on God.

To all the caregivers weary beyond words,
you are the true warriors.

To those battling disabilities,
you are the resilient ones.
You are not disabled... you are Well Able.

CONTENTS

INTRODUCTION

My son Seth was hit by a van while riding his bike, training for a triathlon. He spent five long months in the hospital before eventually coming home in a wheelchair and diapers. This was only the beginning of his arduous journey of recovery. He had to relearn the most basic skills, though the doctors warned us he would not have much success. In fact, they didn't think he would survive.

We are grateful for the team of doctors and medical staff that was (and continues to be) a part of Seth's recovery, but they were limited to the scientific confines of a medical journal. Where science is forced to put a period, God steps in. Through Seth's story, I have learned that miracles happen outside the margins. The God-factor part of Seth's story proves Jehovah God is a healer.

This book highlights my son's difficult but incredible recovery journey. Though he died twice on the scene, Seth was revived and set on a life-altering, all-encompassing course. His story not only proves you can survive unexpected tragedy, but you can also thrive. As a caregiver and mother, this book also highlights my story within Seth's. Both our lives have been forever changed by an unimaginable accident that happened on an ordinary day.

Whether you are fighting to overcome an injury or diagnosis or you are a caregiver of someone in the fight for recovery, I pray our story encourages and inspires you to believe. Believe past your own limitations. Believe past the dire prognosis or diagnosis you or your loved one may have received. Most of all, I pray it gives you what I so desperately needed: hope. Seth has been able to prove medical science wrong time and time again. His recovery and ongoing progress, even amidst the setbacks that sometimes occur, is proof that you can overcome if you fight and continue to *Push Through It.*

Blessings,
Kimber Hanchey-Ogden

Chapter 1

SOUL SCARS

"The only scars in Heaven, they won't belong to me and you
There'll be no such thing as broken, and
all the old will be made new
...the only scars in Heaven are on the
hands that hold you now."

— Lyrics from *Scars in Heaven* by Casting Crowns.

Some dates are imprinted on your soul's psyche, altering your life's trajectory. There is some trauma from which you never fully recover. I have learned that trauma does not discriminate. No one is exempt. It doesn't matter your age, race, status, or education—it can happen to anyone at any time and any place. If you live long enough, it will eventually hit you to some degree. When it does, it scars you emotionally, physically, mentally, and spiritually. I call these trauma tattoos or *soul scars.*

They start as *soul wounds*, occurring the moment you receive news so horrific that your mind cannot fully grasp what you're hearing. You feel like you're stuck in an episode of the Twilight Zone, praying to wake up from this horrible nightmare and find your world as it was earlier—beautifully ordinary. The sound of your own voice screaming confirms it's not a dream at all. You're wide awake. It's at that moment, at that place, a *soul wound* invades you, and then, after some time, a *soul scar* is formed.

For the rest of your days, that soul scar can be a catalyst that catapults you back to the past. Like climbing into a time machine from hell, it transports you back to the moment you received the call that brought you the news that would alter your life. The post-traumatic stress resulting from the soul scar can be triggered by something as simple as a song, a sound, a scent, or a season. It suffocates you with fear and anxiety, robbing you of the false sense of security you used to have. Your mundane, predictable life is forever gone.

That was the type of phone call I received on September 28, 2011.

It was a picturesque fall Wednesday afternoon when my (then) husband and I were traveling back to Louisiana from North Arkansas. We had just spent four relaxing days at our cozy cabin nestled atop a mountain—the perfect location to celebrate my birthday. I love the beauty and serenity of nature, and the cabin was a place for me to unwind and regroup. For many years I had homeschooled our three kids and rarely took time for myself. It wasn't until Seth, our youngest, was about 16 that I began to feel like I could get away once in a while. (My oldest, Savannah, was married by this time, and Sierrah was already working full-time as a nurse.) So, for four days, I enjoyed my birthday getaway, just my husband and I, at our peaceful, little mountain retreat. The time flew by as most vacations do. Before we knew it, the four days were over, and it was time to get back to everyday life.

While we were en route heading back home to Ruston, Louisiana, my cell phone rang. It surprised me that I had cell service since we were still out in the boonies, though earlier, as we drove, our son Seth had called to tell us how his college classes had gone that morning. He was in nursing school, and one of the class's activities was participating in a blood drive that day. Seth, however, never ended up having his blood drawn because he was busy tending to some of his fellow students who had passed out or needed fluids or comfort. (Later, we would discover that it was an unforeseen gift from God that Seth had not given blood that day. He would lose so much blood from the accident that, had he donated at the blood drive, he would have been too depleted and would not have survived.) But now, as we continued on our journey toward home, our middle daughter, Sierrah, was calling us. I promptly picked up–

Some dates are imprinted on your soul's psyche, altering your life's trajectory.

"Hey, Sierrah."

"Mom! Seth's been hit–"

"What? What did you say?"

My 19-year-old daughter's voice alarmed me. She was frantic. It was hard for me to understand her through her tears and screams, and to make matters worse, the phone service was spotty on this stretch of the road. Her voice cut in and out, so her message was cryptic: "Seth...hit on his bike...airlifted to Shreveport...they don't know if he's alive...!"

In slow motion, that phone call instantly inflicted one of several *soul wounds* in me that, in time, would leave massive *soul scars*. I couldn't fully compute what my daughter was telling me and what it all meant. For several grueling hours, I would have no idea how severe my son's condition was, whether or not he was even still alive, and, if he was, what the extent of his injuries would be.

Shaking from the news, I called the hospital, but I couldn't get anyone there to give me answers. They didn't have Seth's name at that point. He had not taken his ID with him on his ride. When the state trooper first came on the scene, they found Seth's cell phone, but since it was passcode-locked, they could not find his name or anything about him, so they airlifted him to the trauma center as a "John Doe." Sierrah had found out that an accident had occurred because she called his cell phone about thirty minutes after he left the house. The state trooper had it in his possession by that time.

Sierrah had asked Seth not to go on such a long bike ride that day, but he was adamant. "We need to go shopping for Mom's birthday gift," she reminded him. "Besides, I have a really bad feeling about this." With his dad and me out of town, Sierrah felt responsible for Seth and was uncomfortable about him going such a distance, but he wouldn't listen. She grabbed his arm as he continued to walk out the door, reiterating what she was feeling and adding, "Seth, do not leave!" He smiled his sheepish grin at her and said, "I won't be long."

It wasn't long after Seth took off before the strange feeling in Sierrah's gut intensified, and she decided to give him a call. When she did, a man answered. At first, Sierrah thought it was

Seth trying to be funny and told the male voice on the other end to stop joking. The serious voice identified himself as "Officer *So-and-so*"--she didn't catch his name, but when he asked what her relationship was with the person who owned the phone, she knew something terrible had happened. After telling him she was his sister, he continued. "Well, he's being lifted right now into the medivac. He was hit by a van." When she asked if he was alive, he said he didn't know, but it didn't look hopeful.

When Sierrah called us, we were at least an hour and a half away from home. From there, it would be another hour and fifteen minutes to the Louisiana State University Hospital in Shreveport, where the trauma center was located. After getting nowhere with the hospital or police as to what was happening, I instinctively began texting and calling friends and family asking for prayer. My hand shook as I held the phone. My heart pounded so loudly I could almost hear it. Though I knew little of what was happening, I understood enough to know that Seth desperately needed prayer support. Prayer was not something our family merely engaged in during an emergency. We are Spirit-filled Christians, and our faith has always been our way of life. Calling out to God was our normal daily rhythm, but at that moment, I sensed an overwhelming urgency to be heard by God en masse. So, I started reaching out, gathering the troops, and asking them to pray. Our family, church family, and friends sprung into action and helped Seth fight his battle by getting on their knees on his behalf. I prayed Psalm 118:17 out loud as we drove, inserting Seth's name into the verse: "Seth will not die; instead, Seth will live to tell what the Lord has done." Over and over again, I uttered those words as a declaration, a prayer.

Though I knew God was present, my deep feeling of urgency from the moment I heard from my daughter was mixed with a large dose of panic.

Seth's dad had the same sense and began to drive like he was vying for first place in the Indy 500. Our impressive (though illegal) pace caught the attention of an Arkansas state trooper, and we were pulled over for speeding. So much of what took place at this point remains a blur, but I do know that we were somehow able to communicate enough of the situation to the officer that he put a call in and found out that a young man had, indeed, been airlifted to the trauma center. (Without having ID on him, the medics assumed Seth was about 25 years old, not 17.) We were not slapped with a ticket that day; instead, we were given a police escort to the Louisiana State Line. We drove first to our home to drop off our dogs, who were in the car with us, then straight to the hospital to see our son and get some answers. I still couldn't compute what was happening. My mind raced. I struggled to think rationally.

When we finally arrived at the hospital, we were met by Sierrah and my mother. The pair had arrived thirty minutes before us. At this point, it had been three hours since I received Sierrah's call, and we still knew next to nothing about what had happened to Seth or what condition he was in. We were desperate for answers, but all Sierrah and my mom could tell us was that Seth was in surgery, and his chances of survival were uncertain.

We soon learned that Seth had set out on a 60-mile bike ride as part of his training for an Ironman triathlon. As he rode along a straight and wide section of a four-lane highway on a

The mangled remains of Seth's bike on the highway

Seth slammed the vehicle's hood and caved it's windshield

clear and sunny day, he was struck from behind by a van driven by an 81-year-old woman. Later, more details would emerge. For instance, we would find out that the impact of the collision sent Seth flying backward 167 feet before landing on the second bridge located on that stretch of the four-lane highway. The force of the crash could have easily launched him over the concrete guardrail and into the water below. Had this happened, he would have drowned. Instead, his body was stopped by the guardrail. He was unconscious when he landed, sitting propped up against the rail with his mangled bike lying next to him.

A state trooper, followed by a firetruck, soon arrived at the scene. The fire truck was carrying two EMT students doing their "ride-a-longs." We later learned two essential factors (and obvious provisions from God): first, those EMTs had their kits with them, which included a manual resuscitator called a bag valve mask or BVM. This equipment and their fast action were instrumental in saving his life. The BVM is able to quickly force-feed oxygen into the lungs. Time was crucial, and this apparatus kept him from losing oxygen to his brain. Seth coded twice on the scene and was revived by these EMTs before the helicopter arrived to airlift him to the trauma center. Secondly, the aircraft was able to come as fast as it did because it had just refueled after an emergency run. It was ready to go when the call about Seth's accident came in. Again, time was crucial due to the severity of Seth's brain trauma, and the pilot made it onto the scene and took Seth to the trauma center without delay. (I call things like him not giving blood earlier that day, the guardrail placed where it was, the EMTs being specifically equipped for what Seth needed, and the helicopter having just been fueled, "kisses from heaven." These are signs that God is present and involved in the details, and you'll see them throughout this story. As you read Seth's story, I challenge you to recognize some "kisses" in your own story).

Once the helicopter landed at the trauma center, Seth was immediately taken to emergency surgery for a craniotomy, which meant they would remove part of the bone from his skull. This would expose his brain and relieve pressure from his brain swelling, which could cause further damage or even death. The surgery was in progress when Seth's dad and I arrived at the trauma center, though I couldn't fully grasp what all this meant then. I couldn't think rationally. It all felt surreal, and I was more than ready to wake up from this cruel and confusing nightmare.

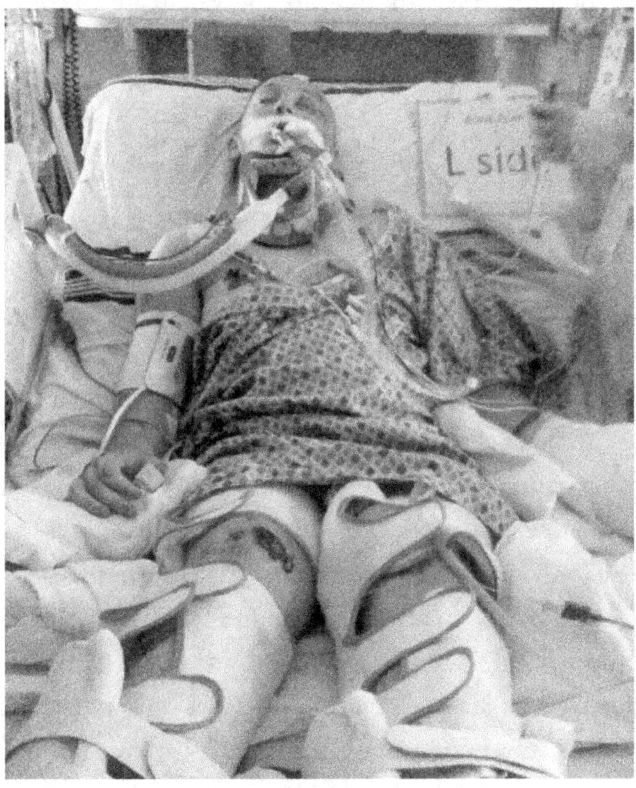

Seth in ICU following initial surgery

After surgery, we were told that Seth's "hemisphere had shifted and his brain stem herniated." This was just the beginning of medical terms we would be hit with that left us dazed and confused. We soon learned that we needed to ask many questions. We were only beginning to learn how life-threatening his diagnosis was and how crucial the next 24 hours would be. Sierrah, next to us listening to the doctor, knew exactly what those terms meant. As a registered nurse, she knew and understood much more of the medical jargon than we did. She wisely kept it to herself, though, and only educated us once Seth passed this critical period. (Sometimes, a little ignorance is a gift.) Seth was still alive, but they didn't expect him to survive the night. He had sustained a severe traumatic brain injury and was in a coma.

Standing at the trauma center when I could go in and see Seth, I felt like I had an out-of-body experience. My mind was reeling. *How can this be? This cannot be happening!* I stood by the bedside of my precious son, who only hours earlier had shared his excitement over beginning his clinicals in the LPN course. As the beeping and rhythmic noises of the machines filled the room, I was overwhelmed with emotions. I was flooded with memories of his childhood and how easy it had been back then to kiss a boo-boo and make the pain disappear. I longed to pick him up and rock him in my arms. If only it were as simple as that. But all I could do was trust God and pray hard. I stayed by Seth's side each time I was permitted into the ICU room. I watched him as he lay there, waiting and wondering. I questioned God as I continued to pray. I questioned the doctors, too. I wanted them to understand that I would be a very present advocate for Seth. They didn't have to like me, but they'd have to deal with me because I was determined to ensure he would have the best care.

Three weeks later, when he was transferred to the Children's Hospital in New Orleans, I began a coping ritual that would last for months. I would steal away to the lavatory in his room, gather all the towels, wad them up onto the floor, and lay down in the fetal position, burying my face in them. Then I would cry and scream into the towels in an attempt to release my pain, frustration, and sorrow. Of course, such things are not so easily released, but still, I tried...many times over. I longed for relief from my wounds, which were deep because my love for my son was immeasurably profound.

Soul scars were inevitable, though my wounds would remain gaping and vulnerable for a long time.

Chapter 2

MARKED FOR GREATNESS

*"A child of God should be a visible beatitude
for joy and happiness, and a living doxology for
gratitude and adoration."*

— Charles Spurgeon

"God has placed greatness inside of you." Those words were spoken over Seth countless times from the moment he was born and first placed into my arms. By how he lived his life, it was evident he believed them. Day after day, he remained in a coma. Sitting by his side in the hospital, I thought about my son and our life with him.

Seth had always lived life fiercely, and I discovered early on that he loved to be challenged. He seemed to be wired for it, and he was competitive. All I had to do to get him to complete a task in record time was tell him one of his sisters had already completed it and mention how long it took her. Then he would tackle it with wild abandon, determined to beat her time.

That same tenacity is how he completed all his homeschool curriculum by age 15, had his diploma in hand at 16, and was enrolled in college to become a nurse by the time he turned 17. (I already knew this innate tenacity would be tested in uncharted and unimaginable ways if Seth woke up from his coma, but it also gave me a small measure of hope.)

Baby Seth

Seth was passionate about helping others. He planned to combine his love for people with his sense of adventure and use his degree to explore the world as a travel nurse. We encouraged him to have a vocation outside of church ministry, but we assumed he would eventually take over as senior pastor of our church someday. He had been groomed for the pulpit and showed a sincere passion and gift for shepherding others as a pastor. Growing up in church watching his dad, myself, and others preach the Word and serve our community, Seth was given models at a young age. He was a very articulate young man and loved expanding his vocabulary. When Seth was about eight years old, he walked around with a small Merriam-Webster dictionary in his back pocket! He loved to look up words and incorporate them into his vocabulary. Seeing this little kid so enthralled with words was comical but also impressive. He spoke with authority, passion, and sincerity. His stage presence commanded people's attention in the most winsome and inviting way. We nurtured and affirmed Seth in these things because it was evident that the Lord had created him with extraordinary gifts and abilities. We had no doubt that God wanted him to use them for His purposes.

It was ingrained in Seth from an early age to respect all people. He was taught they were God's precious creations, regardless of social status or skin color. They were made in His image. Christ valued them so much that He died for them. Seth

> "God has placed greatness inside of you."

understood that as a Christian, it was important to show grace and reflect that same love for all people; even at a young age, he lived that out.

In August of 2000, Seth's father and I founded the first interracial church in our region of Louisiana. At the time of the accident, Seth served as a full-time youth pastor in addition to being a nursing student. He led a group of about 30 kids, ages 11-17. Though many were his peers, Seth was wise beyond his years and dedicated to studying Scripture. When he was with the youth group, he taught them God's Word and led them in fun and meaningful group activities. As a church, we were all about street outreach, so we went to where people lived—on the other side of the tracks, among the crack houses and disenfranchised.

Seth went right along with us. He learned early on to speak up for those with no voice.

Fighting for social justice takes courage, and Seth was as bold as a lion. He was not intimidated by anyone. When he was about 13, he wanted to join us (and over 15,000 others) at the Jena Six protest in Jena, Louisiana. With passion and conviction, Seth marched with us to support the six black students who were excessively and racially discriminated against. We taught him through our words and actions that silence is compliance. To turn a blind eye and say nothing in the face of injustice would make him as guilty as the perpetrator. He had a heart for the underdog and knew doing the right thing would cost him sometimes, but it would be easier than paying the price of living as a coward. Knowing he did the right thing, especially in the face of adversity, allowed him to look at himself in the mirror and respect the reflection staring back. Seth knew he could not expect anyone else to respect him if he didn't respect himself. This was who my son was. And I couldn't have been more proud.

Confident, charismatic, and charming—these words described Seth, and as parents, we were grateful. But sometimes, his dad and I would be forced to butt up against his confidence head-on. Like most teenagers, he was convinced he knew more than we did. He loved to debate with us, which drove me crazy at times (and still does)! Many nights he'd come into our bedroom and want to have a deep conversation late at night when his dad and I were ready to end our day and go to sleep. Though I didn't always appreciate his timing, I did love that he felt free to engage with us in this way. He asked us questions and freely offered his own thoughts and opinions. He would also get talking and often let something slip, telling on himself and confessing something he'd done before we found out about it through someone else! And he was always up to something.

Seth loved to laugh, tell jokes, and play pranks on his closest friends and family. Once he set his mind on pulling a prank, he was committed to seeing it through, which was admirable and infuriating. One that quickly comes to mind happened when he was 12 years old and about fifty of us were on a family cruise. Seth had already been reprimanded several times as we sailed along the ocean. As a result, he was well-known among the crew. But when we docked at a port and were supposed to disembark the ship, no one in our family could find him. I was more angry than worried. *What is he up to now?* Since we were a large group, we equipped ourselves with walkie-talkies so we could communicate when we were apart.

I put out a "distress call" to the family, asking if anyone had seen Seth. Finally, after an hour of searching for him on the ship, my brother announces over the walkie-talkie that he found him. How he managed to disembark without a parent, I'll never know. But there he was, hanging out at the end of the pier. As soon as I got to him, I grabbed him by the arm and proceeded to spank his behind in perfect rhythm with every word I said. I screamed in a loud, stern momma's voice, "I. Don't. Care. If. I. Go. To. Jail. In. Mexico. Today!" (*Would they arrest a mom for spanking her kid in this country?* I had no idea!) The two of us were going in a circle as I was spanking him. What a sight we must have been! My brother, who was still next to Seth, said, "I didn't want to have to tell you this, but he has a tattoo on his arm." My jaw dropped as I looked down at Seth's arm to find a Chinese symbol tattoo. It was fresh—swollen and pink around the ink. I was livid! I wondered how this would go over at church—the pastors' kid, not yet a teenager, with a tattoo. But the joke was on me.

The ink on his tattoo was henna, so it was temporary, though it looked permanent due to his reaction to the henna. The "ink" was raised, adding to the effect that the tattoo was real. Seth pulled off his prank for two weeks, blackmailing his sisters to help him refresh his tattoo each day with a Sharpie, and kept us all convinced that he had snuck out and gotten a real tattoo in Mexico. His commitment to the joke was both impressive and maddening, to say the least. That was how Seth rolled, being all in, even with a stupid prank! He also loved to embarrass Savannah and Sierrah, and sometimes the three of them joined forces and had a lot of fun being silly together. Seth was the ringleader in most scenarios and was always the center of attention—even in a room full of strangers.

Like most 17-year-olds, he was also full of himself. At the time of his accident, he was 5'6" and about 170 pounds. Yet, he considered himself to have the sex appeal of Casanova and the swagger of James Bond! Girls in his nursing class enjoyed his company. They told me that Seth was ever the gentleman. He would carry their books to their cars and insist they call or text him when they arrived home safely. They appreciated his hugs and would ask him for dating advice, though he wasn't dating anyone at the time. When he discovered that some of his class-mates were involved in unhealthy, dysfunctional relationships,

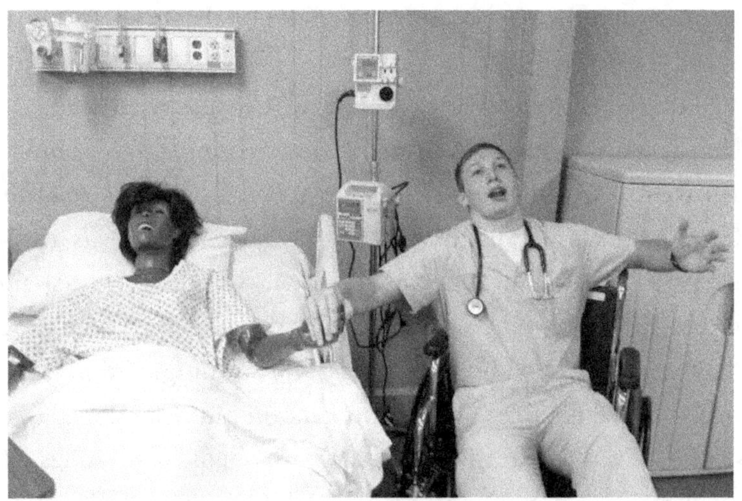

Seth clowning around in nursing school

Seth's senior picture

he encouraged them to raise their standards and refuse to accept abuse or disrespect.

Seth was always on the lookout for his next adventure. I guess you could say he was an adrenaline junkie. He would be inspired by something he'd see on a T.V. show or a YouTube video and declare, "I'm going to do that!" Because he was driven and goal-oriented, he'd usually go for it–whatever it was–and we'd be forced to support him or get out of his way! Seth especially enjoyed rock climbing, free-style running, and parkour. He also loved biking, but he didn't take stupid risks. The day he was hit, it was a beautiful clear day with visibility for miles. He was wearing a helmet and his white biking jersey. His reflective light, mounted at the rear of his bike, was clearly visible. However, none of those things did much for him on the day of his accident.

I thought of all these things and more as I stared at my boy lying in his hospital bed. My vibrant, handsome son's body was bruised, gashed, and swollen. There was a chunk missing from his skull, and he was on a ventilator (they would transition him to a trach a week later). He was hooked up to a myriad of monitors, and IVs fed his body the medications and fluids he needed to survive, and yet there was no guarantee that he would. How could this be my child? How could God let this happen to him? He had been so full of life and had so much more to live.

Seth remained in a coma for ten days. And then he woke up—sort of.

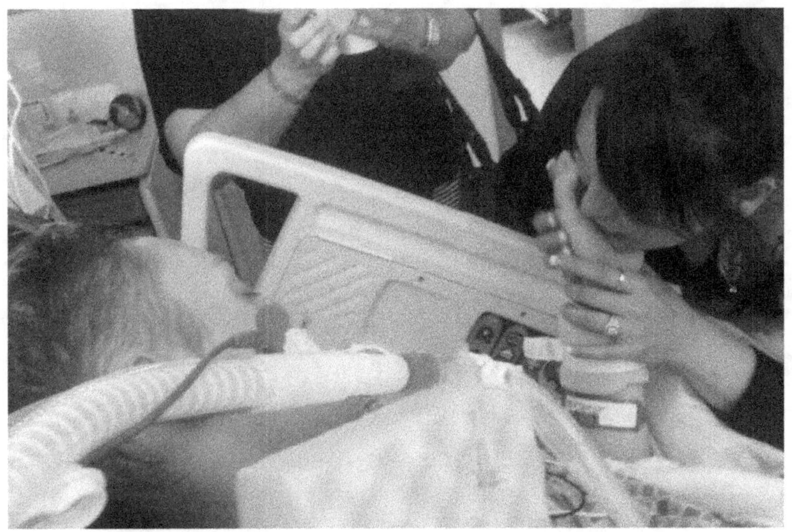

Seeing Seth in a coma was so emotional. I put his hand to my face wishing there was a way I could just hold my baby.

Chapter 3

SPEAKING LIFE

*"Pleasant words are like a honeycomb, sweet and delightful
to the soul and healing to the body."*

— Proverbs 16:24 (AMP)

Every time I was able to see Seth in the ICU, I spoke life and purpose over him. On day ten, he was still unresponsive and in a coma. As I held his hand, God gave us a sign. I said, "You're going to do great things for God, Seth Cole," and he responded by squeezing my hand three times.

To say we were thrilled is an understatement, but our praise party was cut short. It turns out that while Seth had technically come out of his coma, he was in a state of minimal consciousness. After he had responded to my words, one of Seth's doctors took us across the hall to talk. We were expecting to hear how great it was that he responded and how this was a sign of a positive outcome. Instead, we were told Seth's brain was so damaged that he would remain in a vegetative state for the rest of his life. She explained further that if a vegetative state persists, only 25% of patients live more than five years, and most die within six months of the initial brain damage.

Before he squeezed my hand, letting me know that he was

emerging from the depths of his coma, we experienced another incident that, for a split second, seemed to indicate that he was coming out of it. It took place the first night he had been brought to the trauma center and underwent surgery. Though it turned out he was still in a coma, the incident brought with it celebration, nonetheless. It happened while I was with my mom and sisters in the hospital waiting room. I had fallen asleep on one of the chairs and dreamed that Seth was reaching out for me and calling out, "Mom!" The dream was so vivid that I reached back for him and cried out his name as I was startled awake. At that moment, Seth's dad ran into the waiting area yelling, "He just sat up and was reaching!" He then described the scene I had just experienced in my dream. Even though Seth remained comatose, this dramatic movement gave us some important news.

When he sat up, it told the doctors that his spine was not severed. Before this, they had focused only on his brain trauma and assumed Seth was paralyzed. His back had been ripped open from the accident—it was severely gashed, and a lot of sand and dirt was embedded in the wound. Amazingly, the deep gash that occurred when he was struck by the van and landed on the cement guardrail started on the top of his left shoulder, jumped his spine, and continued down to the right side of his waist. Had it affected his spine, he undoubtedly would have been paralyzed.

Of course, hearing that he sat up was encouraging news, but what I pondered in my heart at that moment was the supernatural gift God had given me in the form of a dream. Here was one of those *kisses from heaven*. From a different room, behind a door, and down the hall, God had allowed me to see my son reaching for me. The Lord met me in my sleep with this gift, and He would meet me countless other times when I was awake and very actively trekking through this journey He had us on. I was thankful and blown away by this sign of God's kindness toward me. Still, it was a constant fight to keep the faith and not give in to believing the negative "inevitable" outcome the doctors told us to expect.

Each day brought with it bad news. I was committed to speaking life and healing over Seth, but sometimes I struggled to believe what I was saying. What I saw with my natural eyes was the opposite of what I spoke in faith. My faith and fear constantly wrestled with one another. I wanted to have faith in God. I wanted to believe that somehow, some way, this would all turn around, but the irrefutable medical evidence presented daily said otherwise. With every scan, every consult, every report, and every setback, my fears threatened to smother my faith.

I fought to hold onto my faith, but the doctors' reports mocked my stance. Their words replayed over and over in my mind like a broken record. Yet, as a family, we held on. We were so adamant in our belief that God would turn all of this around that the hospital sent a psychiatrist in to tell us we were in denial! He offered to counsel us to help us learn to accept our reality. The truth is, faith can make you look crazy when you believe in the impossible.

Still, even in my sincere stance of faith, my emotions would permeate and threaten to overtake me. I fought to hide my tears and my fears from Seth. I held it all in until I knew he was asleep. Then, I would slip into the bathroom in his hospital room for my nightly ritual of piling up all the towels onto the floor and screaming and crying into them. Sometimes all I could do was groan because I was so weary and distraught from the day's events. Night after night, I poured out my pain and prayed for God to heal my son.

Three weeks after the day of his accident, now that Seth was "awake" and stable enough, he was transferred to New Orleans Children's Hospital. This felt like a positive move in the right direction, but the grim prognosis that he would be in a perpetual vegetative state for the rest of his life continued to envelop me. His first neurologist at the trauma center had told us that the severity of Seth's injury meant that he ranked as low as he could go on the "Rancho Los Amigos Scale" without being dead. (This scale is a clinical tool used to rate how people with brain injuries recover.) I thought about her words as she told us matter-of-factly that, essentially, Seth was beyond hope. She advised us to institutionalize our son, stating that we were not equipped nor trained to provide the around-the-clock care he would require. Caring for him ourselves, in her estimation, was impossible. I didn't have to think long about her words. I wouldn't even consider them. Institutionalizing Seth was not an option; thankfully, his dad and I were in complete agreement over this. I took care of him from the moment he began to grow in my womb. So, if this continued to be my life's purpose, I would take care of him for the rest of my days.

He would need his trach cleaned out, his feeding tubes inserted, his diapers changed, and much more. "Do you see the complexities?" the doctor persisted. "You need to go ahead and look for an institution to put him in." My response to her was adamant. "I changed his diapers before, and I can do it again!" And that was that. (However, I understand that not everyone can care for their loved one. I don't share this part of our story to inflict guilt on anyone who may need to put their child, spouse, or loved one into an institution. I simply knew that not only was I compelled to take care of Seth, but I was also convinced in my heart and mind that I could do it. God called me to do it, and He would sustain me.)

I received more information through a specialist one Sunday morning when he led me to a conference room to talk about Seth. The room was aesthetically cold and dark, which turned out to be the perfect setting for the devastating meeting we were about to have. In the middle of the room was a long, wooden table. In the corner were three items: a computer, a plastic model of the brain, and a pointer stick. The doctor led me over to the table and invited me to sit down. On his computer, he showed me a brain scan. He nonchalantly told me that this was Seth's brain and then proceeded to inform me (as if I was a medical student and not the mother of a son with a traumatic brain injury) of a long list of things Seth would never be able to do again. The doctor's approach caught me off guard. It was blunt and unfeeling, and I was in shock. After a week and a half at the trauma center, I was also beyond exhausted. There are no words to describe the state I was in. Exhaustion is layered during trauma, so I was already moving about in a fragile, this-can't-be-happening, depleted state. It was like I was slogging through Jell-O and thick fog at the same time. My weariness extended from the surface of my body to the core of my soul.

I ached emotionally, mentally, spiritually, and physically.

And now, all the "nots," "nevers," and "won'ts" the doctor was piling on threatened to completely undo me. I was pummeled, crushed by the weight of them. He began to explain that when the brain is injured, it doesn't heal like a broken arm or leg. It withers up and dies. As he pointed to the milky white area on the brain scan, he explained that this was the damaged part of the brain that was now filled with water and was forever gone. Then he said, "He's not going to have his sight. He'll never walk or talk again. He won't understand humor. He's not going to have memories. He won't know who you are or even who he was...." He went on and on. *Please, God, make him stop. Let me wake up from this nightmare.*

I couldn't speak. No words came. But a faucet was turned on inside me, and I silently cried a steady stream of tears. They poured down my face, and I couldn't stop them, let alone wipe them away. I was in a daze looking at that computer screen. So I let my tears overtake me, drenching me with sorrow as questions and thoughts swirled in my head: *"How can this be happening? My son's brain is gone and will never return. How am I going to fix this? If you take someone's memories, they won't be the same person inside. It's the experiences that make us who we are. Seth won't know who he is. He won't know me. He won't remember our vacations, laughing with his sisters, the silly pranks he pulled on friends, his accomplishments...His past is gone, and now his future is gone."*

I left that awful conference room and somehow found my way back to Seth's room despite my muddled state of mind. The only reason I felt I could leave Seth to meet with the doctor in the first place was because he was asleep. (As days turned into months in the hospital, we made sure that a family member was always with him, especially when he was awake. Twice during his hospital stay, because one of us was present, we were able to quickly alert the medical staff of an issue he was having. He would have died without immediate attention if we hadn't been there at that exact moment.) As I reentered Seth's room and confirmed that he was still sleeping, I quietly pulled the curtain that separated his bed from the window seat, which I had made into my sleeping quarters. (I had brought a full-size egg crate mattress topper and folded it in half to create some cushion on the rock-hard window seat for a makeshift bed.) There I sat for a few moments, completely numb.

I couldn't wrap my head around any more bad news. It just kept coming and coming like one tidal wave after another. I needed to come up for air before I drowned. So, I silently slipped into the bathroom and did the only thing I could at that moment: I wadded up all the towels, dumped them onto the floor, laid myself on the ground in a fetal position with my face buried in terry cloth, and screamed and cried. I also cursed God. *"How can You allow this to happen to my son? He was doing nothing wrong. He was pursuing the call You put on his life! What about those people who have molested someone or killed someone? What about them? Punish them! Not my son."* After allowing myself this meltdown for several minutes, I stood up, splashed my face with water, and sat back down in my window seat. All the while, Seth continued to sleep.

As I worked to control my breath and further compose myself, in walked one of the nurses. My immediate thought was, *Oh, no! What now?* But this woman was one of the precious ones, and her presence quickly comforted me. She tenderly spoke words of life to me at that moment, and I will be forever grateful for her. All hope had been sucked out of me at this point, and I was left to suffocate, but then this nurse entered my space and resuscitated me with her words. She said, "I know what the doctor told you, and I know how hard this is and how impossible it looks, but I can tell you what I've seen, not medically or statistically what doctors will tell you, but I've seen things...." She proceeded to tell me of miracles she witnessed in patients she had encountered. God knew I was starving for hope, so he sent this nurse to me. In that brief conversation, she gave me a crumb of hope that seemed like a banquet.

> *Rest assured, God can handle your temper tantrums and soul-wrenching laments.*

If you're suffering from an injury, have been given a dire diagnosis, or if you are the caregiver of a loved one in a similar situation, I pray the words in this book speak life to you. I pray they will provide you with at least a morsel of hope that helps sustain you at this time. Maybe they will even fill you like the satisfying meal provided at a banquet spread. As you read, partake!

Like us, you most likely have experienced a variety of milestones and setbacks in the journey you are on. As our story unfolds in these pages, I hope you will receive a clear picture of the Savior we've looked to—though imperfectly—in our lives before and after Seth's accident. His name is Jesus Christ. Though there had been many moments of anger, sadness, and resentment, we know full well He has never left our side. He has met our needs and strengthened our faith at our most depleted times. Rest assured, God can handle your temper tantrums and soul-wrenching laments. He's not offended by your lack of faith or the shaking of your fist. He's bigger than that. He's greater than that. He is speaking life to you. Can you hear Him? He's full of compassion for you. And not only can He handle your "whys," but He invites you to bring them to Him. I can attest to this.

Chapter 4

WHY, GOD, WHY?

"When we honestly ask God the 'why' question, He doesn't give us answers as much as He gives us Himself."

— Joni Eareckson Tada

As a church girl, I was raised to revere God and to never, ever question Him. My love for God was enormous. My faith in Him was limitless. My trust in His will was without question. But all of that changed on September 28, 2011. When I learned about what happened to Seth, my belief was broken and gnarled, just like the bicycle Seth had been riding when he was hit. My faith was replaced with doubt and fear. How could something so horrific happen to the son God gave me? I had been faithful. If He would allow this, what else might be inflicted on my loved ones down the road?

Fast-forward to when Seth finally came home from the hospital. He had to have someone with him at all times. I couldn't hire support staff to help me with my son, though his needs were significant. I always assumed that when someone was injured to this extent and the other person was clearly at fault, that insurance would compensate. I found this not to be true. The woman who hit him did not even have enough insurance to cover his life flight, much less assist us with the bills that piled up. Thankfully, my mom came by every day to help out— free of charge! Sierrah worked a full schedule with her nursing job but lived at home and helped out when she wasn't at work. Savannah was living on her own an hour away from us. Even though she worked full-time, she helped with her brother as often as she could. Still, with all this support, my daily tasks were insurmountable. I hit the ground running each day and kept the plates spinning and the balls in the air 24/7. There wasn't time to think about it; I just had to do what needed to be done. I may have looked confident and strong, but I was in a fragile state those first months of getting in a groove with Seth. During those days, I looked forward to my showers like never before. It was the only place I felt I could safely let go and fall apart.

I'd retreat to my bathroom and take up my familiar position, weighed down by the flood of emotions. Now that I was home, I curled up on my shower floor instead of the bathroom floor. Sad, angry, and full of despair, bitterness and anguish consumed me. I had never experienced depression and anxiety before, but now I was dealing with both and broadsided some days with panic attacks. As I wept, I longed for the hot water that poured over me to wash it all away. After each episode, I thought I couldn't possibly have more tears left in me to cry, but, of course, they would return. I hated the way I felt. I hated being mad at God. I desperately wanted to find peace and joy in trusting Him again. Ironically, I needed His help to do so.

I could no longer let the monster of anger and bitterness torment me. I had placed myself willingly in a prison that kept me miserable and bound. Living this way only added to my exhaustion. One evening after my nightly ritual of despair, I acknowledged my anger to the Lord and surrendered it. I simply prayed and asked God to forgive me (yet again) for the things I said and for how I felt. I also asked God to help me forgive Him. It didn't happen overnight. It was a process I would repeat many times, and it took years before I could fully trust Him again, but healing came. Forgiveness happened. Surrender is freedom.

Hold Onto Faith

Faith is the substance of things hoped for. True faith exists in spite of emotions. When your faith and fear collide, it's a fight to hold onto faith in God and His purpose for your life.

The enemy (yes, the devil is real, and he is our enemy) strategically plants thoughts in your mind to produce doubt and fear. Like seeds planted in the ground, you can water and nurture those destructive seeds by what you dwell on, allowing them to grow and overtake you. That's why it is essential to guard your mind. Put a stop to wrong thinking (like the "what-ifs" that can paralyze you), and replace those negative thoughts with those mentioned in Philippians 4:8 (NLT): "...Fix your thoughts on *what is true*, and *honorable*, and *right*, and *pure, and lovely*, and *admirable*. Think about things that are *excellent and worthy of praise*." Like tuning into the correct channel on the radio, whichever way you turn the dial strengthens one voice over the other. What voice are you listening to? Where do your thoughts go?

It takes effort to tune out destructive thoughts and dial into the faith-filled ones. And even if you do that well, it doesn't mean you won't struggle. Have you ever asked God, "WHY?" If so, I want you to know you're not alone. I wrote the following in my journal when Seth was in New Orleans Children's Hospital three months after his accident:

This weekend has been a trying one. Seth's mental battle has been difficult because he IS so 'aware.' The awareness is actually a good thing, though also a tormenting one. He is angry, frustrated, and even battling depression because he cannot walk, talk, or even go to the bathroom. I said, "I know you are asking God WHY this happened to you." He kissed the top of my hand and began to cry. It broke my heart.

> Anyone can fight a battle that lasts for a day or a week. But when the battle stretches into months or years, even the strongest warrior gets weary and feels like giving up.

It's okay to ask God, "Why?". I had a heart-to-heart with Seth that day (and many days following) and reminded him of his favorite scripture, Romans 8:28. I told him, "Even when you can't see it, all things are still working together for the good of those who love Him and are called according to His purpose! I have learned and relearned to have confidence in the *Who*, even when I don't understand the *why*. I still believe that what the enemy sent to destroy you, God will turn around and work it for your good. That's how awesome God is. He can take a mess and turn it into a message; this test will become a testimony. So just keep pushing through it, son! Even when you don't understand. You are a warrior, and warriors just keep fighting."

This was more than a pep talk. It was a truth talk for my son as well as for myself. Over the months and years, we engaged in countless interactions like this and still do! Sometimes it was Seth helping me hold on to faith, and sometimes it was my turn. We all need a partner in the journey. Seth's dad was my partner in this for a while, but about a year after the accident, he fell apart, and our relationship crumbled under the stress and strain of the situation. Fire forges or fragments a relationship. The fire we have gone through has forged a bond between Seth and me in the most unbreakable way possible. We have also had many family members, our church family, and other friends surrounding us, for which I am deeply grateful. They have stepped in and offered invaluable prayer and practical support.

Anyone can fight a battle that lasts for a day or a week. But when the battle stretches into months or years, even the strongest warrior gets weary and feels like giving up. If this is you right now, I hope you're finding encouragement in the pages of this book. Whatever you're going through today, DON'T GIVE UP! Just keep going, and you will get through it. One. Day. At. A. Time. Go ahead and ask "Why?" when you need to, but hold on. Don't lose your grip on faith. It will sustain you.

Chapter 5

THE HOSPITAL LIFE

"When suffering happens, it forces us to confront life in a different way than we usually do."

— Philip Yancey

For five months, we had no choice but to deal with what came one day at a time within the walls of the hospital. Seth's hospital room became home base, though there is nothing about that room that I would call "homey." It truly felt like a prison most days. Still, we were thankful that, because Seth was not yet considered an adult, we were able to stay with him around the clock, including the days he spent in the ICU. Let me just say that until Seth's accident, our family had been relatively unfamiliar with hospitals. We hadn't experienced much in the way of medical emergencies or severe injuries. As a small child, Seth had pneumonia twice and spent a night each time in the hospital, but that was about it. The girls were healthy, and Seth's dad and I were healthy. So, though Sierrah worked as a nurse before Seth's brain injury, we were not accustomed to the "hospital life" we were now living.

Even after all the months inside those walls, being in a hospital never became normal. It's a chaotic, aesthetically (and practically) cold, sterile, and depressing place. For as long as Seth had to stay there, I was determined to do whatever I could to make things nicer and create a more inviting atmosphere, primarily for Seth but also for our family. When he woke up in the morning, I'd play upbeat music to start Seth's day on a happy note. (The typical sounds of a hospital with beeping machines or even sterile silence are far from "happy.") As the day progressed, and when relaxing, beautiful music was more appropriate, I'd play that softly in the background instead. A nurse gave us a practical tip to use peppermint oil in a diffuser to get rid of the stench, so I took her advice and placed a diffuser in his room to keep the place smelling less "hospital" and more "home." I brought in soft blankets and items from home to make his room more comfortable.

After that first night in the ICU, we banned crying in Seth's room. Don't get me wrong, I know it's important to grieve, and tears can be cleansing. They are a normal part of life, and we had every right to let them flow under the circumstances. But as a family, we agreed that Seth's room would be a "no-crying zone." (The bathroom, however, with its heavy door, fan, and towels, came in handy to muffle the sound of my loud wailing!) We weren't living in denial, but his room needed to be a place where we spoke life into him and celebrated his existence and small milestones. We could talk about the dire reality of his situation and fall apart if need be outside of his room. But we were determined to offer him a steady stream of words of encouragement and sincere smiles. If tears were shed in front of him, they would be tears of joy.

I found out months later that this conviction of mine that

we not cry in Seth's room was from the Lord. I say this because when Seth got to a point where he could communicate, he told me that he heard us crying while he was in a coma, and he didn't like it. I'm so grateful that without even knowing that fact, we made it a point after his first night to not bawl our eyes out in his room where he could hear or see us. We were committed to promoting an atmosphere of healing, not sorrow.

Leaving Seth in the hospital alone was not an option, so Seth's dad and I established a routine for those five months to ensure that one of us was always by his side. I stayed in the hospital with Seth, sleeping on the window seat in my makeshift bed, from Friday to Monday. Seth's dad would then relieve me and come and stay with Seth the other days, sleeping in the lounge chair in the room at night. Savannah, Sierrah, and other family members and friends would visit as often as possible.

Each day spent within those four walls was generally a blur. Sometimes it felt like we were in our version of the movie Groundhog Day, but this was no romantic comedy. And while there was a lot of downtime in the hospital, there never seemed to be enough hours in the day to do everything we needed to do. Our new life in the hospital was all-consuming, yet our "normal" life outside the building still required our attention.

Seth laid in his hospital bed being treated for his traumatic brain injury and working to recover from his initial wounds and surgery. He then had to recover and heal from the subsequent surgeries—fourteen in the span of five months. It often felt like one step forward, two steps back. Sometimes, three steps back. It appeared to be never-ending, so our prayers for him were never-ending. What also seemed relentless was all the hours of therapy he endured.

I went with him to his physical, occupational, recreational, speech, and music therapy sessions and watched him put in the hard and painful work of recovery at each one. Most days, the sessions didn't seem to be doing much for him other than causing pain. At times the therapies simply highlighted the long list of "nots" and "nevers." Then there were the days we would see the occasional glimmer of hope, though it was just a twinge; it was like a cool drink of water after wandering in the desert.

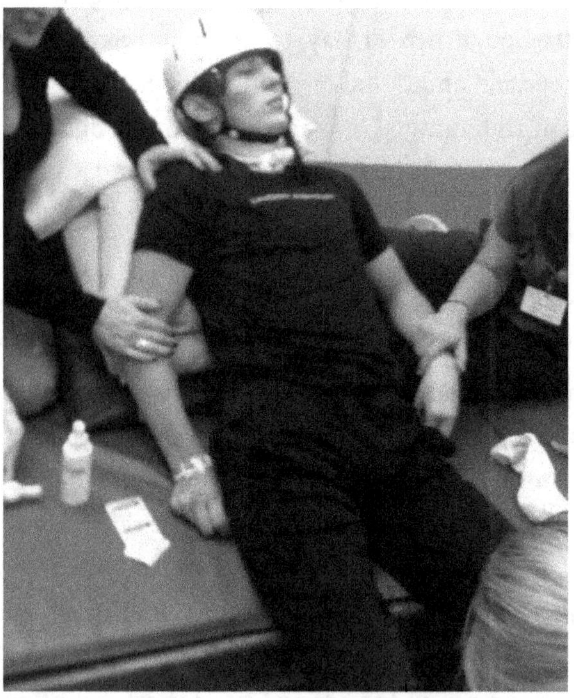

Therapist teaching Seth to sit up using his left hand due to right side paralysis. He had to wear a helmet at all times because part of his skull had been removed.

I remember the milestone we witnessed many months after his accident when Seth held his own spoon and fed himself. In the days that followed, he continued to get more food on his lips and chin than he was able to get into his mouth, but spoonful by spoonful, he began to get the hang of it. This was the second time in Seth's life I celebrated this milestone. (The first when he was still a baby in a highchair.) I could never have imagined or foreseen the scenario we were now experiencing.

During all this, I spent lots of time mulling over how we were going to move forward and function in our new life. I was a wife and momma to two daughters who, although they were adults now, still needed me, and I wanted to maintain my place in their lives. I also had a church congregation to whom I felt called to minister. I wondered how I could juggle these relationships while doing all that must be done for Seth. As I wrestled with this challenge, God opened my eyes to yet another role he wanted me to play. I knew I had been given a new sphere of influence in the hospital's hallways, waiting areas, and patient rooms. God would often prompt me to go up to a grieving parent or a scared or bored child staying alone in the hospital and offer a hug, an encouraging word, and a smile. The Holy Spirit would nudge me to minister to a nurse or other medical staff. Sometimes this felt like sacrificial giving when I was hurting so badly, but I discovered it was a healing balm for me and a blessing to those God led me to. Booker T. Washington is known to have said, "If you want to lift yourself up, lift up someone else." His words reflect Proverbs 11:25 (MSG), which says, "The one who blesses others is abundantly blessed; those who help others are helped." This was my experience.

I had no idea, at the time, of how Seth would live this out in the days ahead as he began to recover. God had a plan for him I had yet to understand. I would also learn that I had a role to play in that plan. It would unfold gradually and take many twists and turns along the way. And the path didn't always move Seth forward. Much of the time, it seemed like there were detours threatening to swallow him up and cut his journey short.

The Impossible Summit

In the hospital, we were met with another setback at some point in each day, followed by yet another bad report. The reports became more and more dire as the list of Seth's limitations grew longer, a constant reminder of the severity of his brain damage. We fought daily to stay positive and keep hope alive, but it seemed like we were facing a mountain higher than Everest.

There's a point on Mount Everest known as the "Kill Zone." There, you will find those who did not survive the climb, monuments forever frozen in time. They serve as a warning to all who dare to attempt the treacherous climb that many will not live through it. They lost sight of the summit. They lost their vision and, with it, their hope. As every climber of Mount Everest will tell you, the air becomes thinner as you ascend in elevation, making breathing harder and more challenging to continue the climb.

Hope is the oxygen you breathe when you are in a crisis. It was our oxygen in the hospital, and we fought to keep it, even when well-meaning medical professionals seemed to suck the hope right out of the room with their grim prognosis. When hope is lost, you feel like you can't breathe, so we continued to do all we could to maintain an atmosphere of hope. The Bible says in Proverbs 13:12 (GNT), *"When hope is crushed, the heart is crushed..."* When we were bombarded with negative reports surrounding Seth's recovery, it felt as though our world was spinning out of control, and there was nothing we could do about it. Our daily lesson was that hope must be fed, especially amid an ongoing crisis. We had to focus on something, anything, positive related to Seth and his journey, no matter how small, and talk it up–for his sake and ours.

> *Hope is the oxygen you breathe when you are in a crisis.*

"Haba Na Haba"

In a time of war, soldiers stay in battle mode. Although such mental preparation is necessary, it takes a toll on their mind and body. The same can be said for those recovering from a debilitating injury or diagnosis. (It can also be said for their caregivers.) You forget to celebrate the wins when you're constantly braced for the next fight. You must discipline yourself to acknowledge the victories, no matter how small. It is disheartening to be so focused on how far you have yet to go that you overlook how far you've already come.

With a brain injury, recovery is a long, daunting process. (In reality, the brain does not recover, it creates new pathways in a process called "synapsis.") The progress is so little at times that it can be missed. Sometimes it takes an outsider's view to give you a true perspective of how well you are doing. We were especially thankful for one of the doctors attending to Seth in the ICU, who said something profound. His words stayed with me while we were in the hospital, and they're with me to this day.

> *You forget to celebrate the wins when you're constantly braced for the next fight. You must discipline yourself to acknowledge the victories, no matter how small.*

He said because brain injury recovery is so slow and each injury is different, you can't compare your recovery to someone else's.

He shared, "In South Africa, where I am from, we say 'Haba na haba,' which means little by little. His progress seems very small to you, but even small progress is progress. It may take many baby steps to get you to the finish line, but the key is to just keep going. Little by little, you will get there."

There's some oxygen! There's the hope we needed!

Whatever your story is, whatever injury you are fighting to recover from, don't make the mistake of comparing your journey to someone else's. Not only can doing so cause you to become self-critical, but it also limits your potential. You'll never go anywhere as long as you focus more on what lies behind you or the life you should've had. It will keep you from ever reaching your goals. You can't drive forward looking in the rearview mirror. It seems automatic to go into a dialogue of negative pillow-talk at the end of the day and mull over what you didn't get right or didn't accomplish. But when you already struggle with your new role as a caregiver (and the learning curve that accompanies it), ruminating on the past further adds to the sense of being overwhelmed and inadequate. I learned the way to counter this and change the narrative in my head was to refuse to spend the last five minutes of my day going over all the things I couldn't change. Rather, I chose to think of all the people I had encouraged that day. It made all the difference to simply take a few minutes to remind myself of all that I did right (not perfect, mind you) and acknowledge it.

You just may be doing better than you realize. Look around you today. Pay attention to the smallest details. It's the little things that add up to be the biggest blessings. Take the time to celebrate every accomplishment, no matter how small, and give God praise. When you focus on the good things, what didn't go right seems less important. *Haba na haba*, my friend. *Haba na haba*.

Discovering Ways to Help

In addition to doing all we could to stay positive, rely on God, and celebrate every tiny spark of progress that brought hope, we also did whatever we could as non-medical professionals to help move Seth's recovery forward. We knew the medical staff was working to help our son, but we would also play an important role. He received a cocktail of meds and therapies throughout the day and night, but we quickly started doing our own research to find out what other things we could do to possibly help Seth.

Starting on day two in the hospital, we made it a point to massage his feet twice a day so he wouldn't get "drop foot." Drop foot is a common issue among people who have suffered a brain injury, and we wanted to combat it from the beginning. It causes them to walk with a limp or prohibits them from walking at all. Even after we were told Seth would never walk again, these foot massages continued as we continued to have hope. Poor Seth hated the massage sessions because they hurt so bad, but we loved him enough to hurt him for the possibility of helping him down the road. Sure enough, it paid off.

We also took the advice of an older nurse who told us to go out and buy Seth a pair of high-top Converse tennis shoes, one size larger than he normally wore. Putting these shoes on him, even while he lay in bed, kept his foot at the most optimal angle to help keep drop foot at bay. We put a bolster pillow at the end of the bed and rested his feet against it to keep them at an optimal 90-degree angle. It may not seem like much, but we believed these "small" things could make a significant difference, so we were committed to trying them.

Another regimen we incorporated into the mainstream treatments the medical staff gave Seth was diet-related. We started feeding him blueberries when his feeding tube was removed three months into his hospital stay. I'm sure he ingested several large vats of blueberries and gallons of blueberry juice in five months! We put them in everything from oatmeal to ice cream! Not only was his mouth stained blue, but his poop was a lovely shade as well! (Nothing remains private for a patient in the hospital!) We made it our mission to supply Seth with these berries when we learned that they are "food for the mind." They reduce inflammation and protect the brain from damage. Studies have shown that blueberries (and other berries) help improve memory, learning, and other

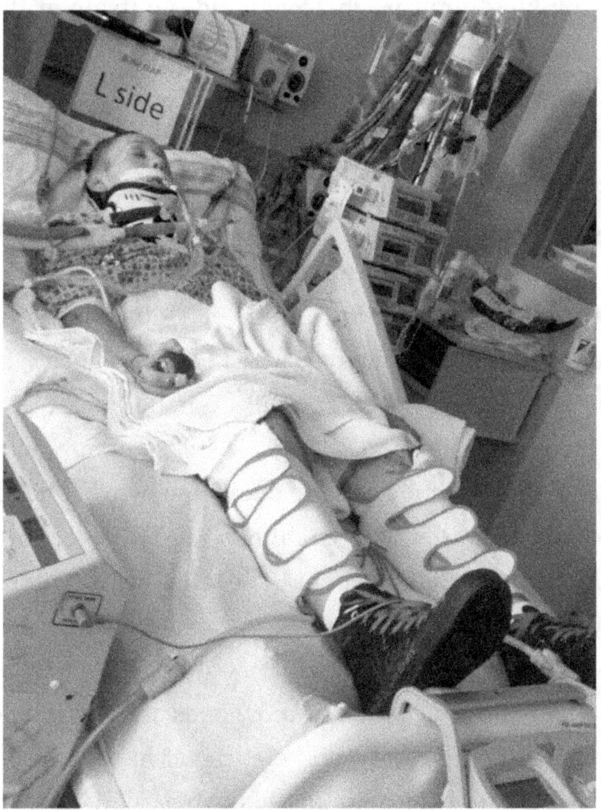

Seth wearing Converse tennis shoes to prevent drop foot

cognitive functions, so we invested a small fortune in these little gems. Thankfully, Seth liked the taste, so it wasn't a fight to get him to eat them.

It helped me and members of our family to feel like we were actively involved in making a difference for Seth, so we constantly looked for new ways to be a part of his recovery process. Our continual presence, verbal and non-verbal encouragement, and insistence that his room remain a positive atmosphere were helpful. Speaking words of life to him, praying for and with him, and taking him for wheelchair rides outside in the fresh air made a real difference. And even playing our version of Uno proved to be beneficial.

It took some trial and error, but we also did the best we could to think ahead and discern what would *not* be a help to Seth. For example, we were careful to not let Seth see himself in a mirror. We felt it would upset him to see what he looked like with part of his skull missing and the left side of his face paralyzed and bruised. But one day, when he was wheeled into the elevator to go to surgery on another floor, he caught his reflection in the shiny, reflective ceiling. He still could not talk at that time, but he was so shocked and overcome by what he saw that he let out a deep, heart-wrenching wail. I'll never forget the sound he made at that moment. It severed my momma's heart and haunted me for some time.

We came to find out several years after Seth's accident that it didn't help him to see photos and videos of himself before the accident. We thought it would help trigger his memory, but he told us years later that he didn't like when we'd try to remind him of who he had been unless he brought it up. Seeing pictures and videos annoyed and frustrated him more than anything. He didn't know the Seth we knew before his accident. He was a stranger to him. (Much later, after some gaps in his memory filled in a bit, Seth said seeing pictures of himself was like looking at a twin brother–it was someone he knew, but it wasn't him. He added, "I like myself better now anyway!") I wish I had understood his feelings earlier, but I had no idea in those early days of his recovery. This is just one example of the learning

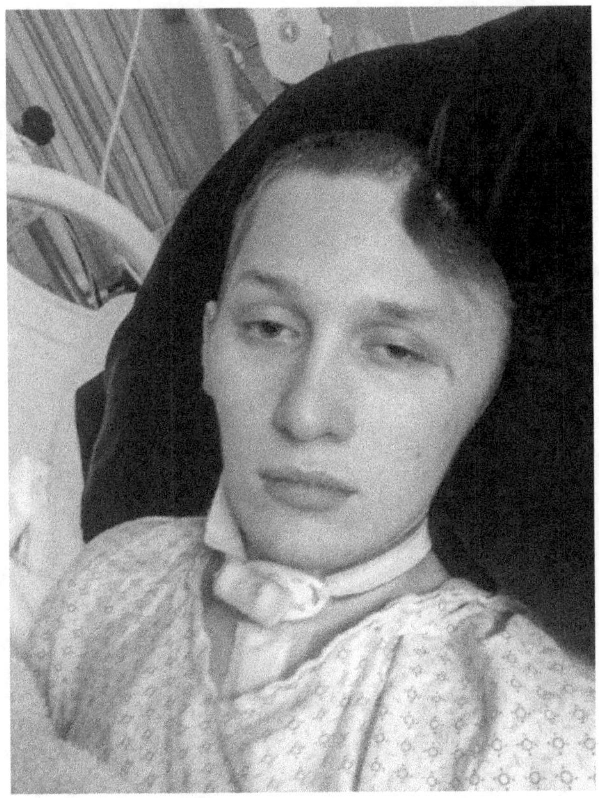

Seth before they replaced his skull piece

curve we were on. As a caregiver, you simply do the best you can, but you can never do it all perfectly.

This was becoming clearer to me: As much as I tried, no one could shield Seth from his physical or emotional pain. He had to walk through it himself, but I would go with him, and most importantly, and much more perfectly, so would Jesus.

Chapter 6

THE VALLEY OF SHADOWS

*"Courage is not simply one of the virtues, but the form of
every virtue at the testing point."*

— C.S. Lewis

Between every mountain lies a valley. As I walked this journey with Seth, for the first time in my life, I understood what Psalms 23 refers to as the Valley of the Shadow of Death. As Seth became more aware of his situation and the days in the hospital continued, this is where Seth was trapped—in an in-between place. Valleys are dark places, and in the darkness, just like when you were a child, your mind can begin to play tricks on you. The fear of the unknown, coupled with your imagination, runs wild. The intimidating shadows quickly become your worst horrors. I had to remember and remind my son—it's only a shadow. It feeds on fear, stealing strength, and crushing the spirit. I couldn't know exactly what Seth was feeling and thinking because he couldn't communicate it to me verbally at this point, but I could read his eyes. His face said so much.

I learned, as never before, that the constant torment of the unknown will wear you down. The enemy is good at filling in the blanks and feeding our fears. His goal is to convince us to give up the fight. He wants us to believe we'll never make it out alive. He will divert our attention from any progress made, overshadowing it with another bad report. His mission is to convince us that we are forgotten and alone. *Why are you even fighting? Just give up.* Perhaps as you read this, you are nodding your head. You can relate to these unrelenting taunts. If so, let me tell you what I told Seth and myself countless times: *Don't fall for it. It's only a shadow. Just keep pushing through, and you'll make it out on the other side. Keep fighting the fight.*

Envisioning

"Believe you can and you're halfway there."
— Theodore Roosevelt

You have to see it before you get there. The Bible says in Proverbs 29:18 KJV, "Where there is no vision, the people perish..." Without a vision for your future, you lose the fight to move forward. You give up on life. You lose sight of meaning and purpose. I did an exercise with my children when they were young that I called envisioning. I would have them close their eyes and visualize their futures in great detail. This exercise proved to be a game changer during Seth's recovery.

Our brains are adept at painting pictures. Envisioning is simply projecting yourself into that image and writing the accompanying narrative. It is essential to be very descriptive when doing this, even down to the most minute detail. This is a powerful tool to help you make subconscious goals that your mind will follow. So, envisioning became part of our nightly ritual. Before Seth went to sleep, first and foremost, I would pray with him. Then, with his eyes still closed and classical or spa-like music playing softly, I guided him with my words as I painted a picture of him in his future. I needed Seth to project himself past his current situation and limitations—past what the doctors said his outcome would be. I needed to give him this anchor to hold onto.

Remember, Seth couldn't even get out of bed at this time. But I told him to get dressed so we could go back and climb the arches at Arches National Park in Utah. I described the gear he was wearing in great detail, from his head down to his five-toe climbing shoes. I described the exquisite view from the top and asked if he could see it. Here Seth was, half his face still paralyzed, listening intently with his eyes closed. When a crooked grin spread over his face, I knew he saw it. (There *were* past memories present in his mind!) Then I said, "Okay, let's change clothes. You have a speaking engagement tonight." I described in great detail the suit he was wearing as he shared his testimony and told how God helped him walk again. I told him he was standing in a large arena before thousands of people. "Can you hear them? Can you hear the roar of praise as you share how God raised you from the dead twice?" I told him thousands of people were being healed, set free, and delivered because of what he overcame.

I challenge you to try this every night for thirty days. Do it for yourself (or for the one in your care). Be creative. Project yourself into your future. What do you see? You write the narrative. Let it be an anchor. Now walk in it.

Push Through It

Three months before the accident, our family took a trip to Utah and visited the Arches National Park. Seth wanted to hike up to the top of the famous Delicate Arch, and he insisted on me going with him. Reluctantly, I gave in.

Halfway up the trail, I was already panting. This was, at best, a three-hour hike with a significant climb and no shade along the way. My 45-year-old, out-of-shape behind sat down and gave up. Yeah, yeah, I know it was hypocritical of me. Here I have always taught my children to never give up—that *can't* was not a word in our vocabulary—and I was doing exactly that. I gave up. I threw in the towel. Whatever you want to call it, the long and short of it was, I quit!

Cue the melodrama as I began listing my excuses. Trying hard to make my case, I said, "I'll only slow you down." I had convinced myself I was going to die on the side of that mountain—in between halfway up and halfway down. I didn't think I had it in me to make it to the top. I tried to convince Seth it would be better to leave me there

> *Quitting lasts forever, pain lasts for a moment, so push through it.*

to catch my breath and that I would be ready to make the trek back down when he returned. I told him, "Go on without me. You can take a picture of the view from the top for me." I'll never forget what he said to me or how profound his words would prove to be just a few months later. He said, "Mom, you'll never get this day back. One day you will regret coming this far and not pushing through to see the view from the top of the mountain with your own eyes. I'm not leaving you behind. You're going to the top if I have to carry you." Then, he leaned over, placed a hand on each of my shoulders, looked me square in the eyes, and said, *"Quitting lasts forever, pain lasts for a moment, so push through it. Now get up, Mom, and push through it!"* He locked his arm underneath mine, and we continued the trek to the top. He was right. A picture would not have been the same as the reward of the view from the summit. It is both a valuable lesson and a memory I will cherish forever.

Those words were his mantra and would be echoed a thousand times over the years to follow in Seth's recovery. Not only by us, but by God.

One day, Seth shared with us about one of those times. It happened when he was still in the hospital and learning to walk again. (He could not articulate any words then, so we learned this well after the fact.) He told us he was in such excruciating pain that he just wanted to give up. At that moment, he said God spoke to him, "Push through it, Seth."

There are challenges many people face in life that are extremely difficult and seem downright impossible. Perhaps that's what you're going through right now, and you're faced with a million reasons to quit. Seth sure was. God may place people on your path to encourage you to press on, but ultimately it is up to you to *push through it.* No one can do it for you. The reward you receive with each summit you crest cannot be achieved by someone else doing it for you. They can't climb for you. They can't see the view for you. You must do it yourself, so you can see it for yourself. This is your life. Your journey. Your story. You have the pen in your hand to write the narrative. Remember, you're not doing it alone. God is with you every step of the way.

A Picture Really Is Worth a Thousand Words

I took a picture of Seth that day as he stood at the top of that mountain underneath one of the most famous arches in the world. I had no idea three months later, it would be hanging on the wall of his hospital room as a reminder to not give up. As I mentioned earlier, the young man in the photo was a stranger to Seth, so posting it in his hospital room didn't affect him like I had hoped it would, but it spoke to my heart. It reminded me that it was my turn to cheer Seth on with his exact words and encourage him to keep climbing.

I continue to reflect on a valuable lesson I learned that day in Utah: Never take an opportunity for granted, especially one that challenges you. It may be the very thing you cling to later in life to remind you that you have what it takes to overcome. Or perhaps it will be a precious memory made with someone you love, a memory you will one day hold dear, and that will get you through a time of sorrow. Seth was right. I would have regretted it for the rest of my life if I had not made that trek to the top with him.

Seth standing under the Delicate Arch

Seth's signature five-toe shoes

Give Me That Mountain

Ironically, one of the doctors used the term 'steep climb' to describe Seth's recovery. It was another example I could add to my *kisses from heaven* list. It reminded me of part of the sermon Seth preached to his youth group the night before his accident. He spoke about Abraham climbing Moriah with his son, Isaac.

"You will never know God as your Jehovah Jireh until you have to climb Mount Moriah with your promise, prepared to sacrifice what you love the most. Know this: God does not assign the journey to climb Mount Moriah to just anyone. He will only give this mountain to those He trusts to carry out His will. Your Moriah is not meant to be a punishment. It is the ultimate trust test. This is where you meet God and come to know Him as your Provider. Only in this place will you come to learn for yourself what God already knows... what you are truly made of."

— Sermon by Seth Hanchey, September 27, 2011

The higher the mountain and the more difficult the climb, the greater the view will be when you get to the top. Take the risk. Don't quit. Most of all, remember the journey is part of the reward.

Let me encourage you today with whatever mountain you're facing with something I wrote to Seth early on during his recovery:

"Every day, I have watched you continue to climb this steep mountain of recovery. There have been many difficult days and setbacks, and still, you climb. I believe there is purpose in this journey. I also believe what awaits you at the top of this mountain is your promise. When you get there, you will fully know not only your weaknesses but also your strengths. Your strengths will only be more evident, and your weaknesses will have a trek straight through them as you continue with each step to conquer them. There's no quit in you, Seth Cole. You have the heart of a lion. I believe in my God, and I believe in you, my son. I am confident you will overcome, and I have no doubt you will conquer this mountain."

— Kimber Hanchey, October 20, 2011

Chapter 7

"OH, GOD!"

Seth had a sincere relationship with God before his accident. Though I can't say for sure what his memory of his relationship with God was like before September 28, 2011, he instinctively seemed to know to call out to God not long after he woke up from his coma. I sat next to Seth's bed in the ICU at the Children's Hospital one night as he was recovering from yet another surgery. His dad was home that evening, and out of his sorrow and desperation, he got on his computer and began drafting an email to God. He used the salutation, *Dear God.* Though he gave some thought to what he wanted to say to God, Seth's dad never intended to hit send. (What was God's email address anyway?)

Nevertheless, it was therapeutic for him to draft an email to the Almighty. Of course, I had no way of knowing this was happening when Seth was sound asleep, lying in his hospital bed following another surgery, and suddenly he blurted out,

"Oh, God!" This was the first time he had spoken since his accident. Shocked, I jumped out of my sleep and ran to his bedside. I said, "Seth, you spoke! You spoke!" And then—silence. I immediately called Seth's dad and told him what had happened. He couldn't believe it! Weeping, he said, "Kimber, I had just typed the words, 'Oh God,' on my computer, and then you called!" We both marveled at this, knowing it wasn't a coincidence but another *kiss from heaven*, a sweet reminder that God was present. He knew everything, and He was letting us know in His unique and loving way. He could see us. One of His names is "El Roi," which means "the God who sees me."

> *Don't get so distracted looking for more significant signs of His presence that you overlook how He orchestrates even the most minute details.*

Seth didn't utter those words again (or any others) for several months.

Later, God would give Seth a prayer language unlike anything he had received before. Not even a traumatic brain injury could keep Seth away from God's love and intimacy! Like a mom of a toddler just starting to talk, I learned to understand many of the words and phrases in his language. I became familiar with what certain sounds, tones, and inflections in his voice meant, and I could interpret them. First thing in the morning, I knew Seth was awake when he began his "conversation with God." This would happen sporadically throughout the day. Seth showed me in the simplest way that it's not about trying to *wow*

God with our elegant speech but merely speaking to Him in our own words and in our own way. This gave me a whole new understanding of the relationship God wants us to have with Him. He calls us friend. He desires that level of intimacy where we tell Him about our day.

Years after he started speaking in his special language, we were at a conference where Seth met a woman who was fluent in several languages. She confirmed for us that his language was not gibberish. He was speaking words but in a language that was his own. She identified that part of his language was Aramaic, describing it as some building blocks of the original language. Seth had never been to the Middle East or exposed to Aramaic. It's certainly not a language he learned when I homeschooled him! In fact, it's considered an "endangered language" and has been almost entirely replaced by Arabic. Yet, after surviving a traumatic brain injury, my son, it seems, was able to speak it to a degree. This was given to him by God, no doubt. Seth also developed a heightened sense of people and their emotions. Time and again, we would witness him ministering to strangers, not from a pulpit but from wherever they showed up on his path and with a very limited vocabulary.

God Is in the Details

I don't know what your situation is at the moment, but I can tell you this: God is not oblivious to it. He is fully aware. He created you. He knows you. And He is in the details of whatever you are going through. Don't get so distracted looking for more significant signs of His presence that you overlook how He orchestrates even the most minute details. I believe it is His way of letting us know He is at work within our lives. The many kisses from heaven we received have served as gentle reminders that He sees us, hears us, and holds us in His hands.

One such kiss from heaven took place almost two years before his accident, back in the summer of 2009, when Seth was just 15 years old. We were on vacation at Jekyll Island State Park in Georgia, and he had gone for an evening run along the beach. When Seth returned, he told us God physically knocked him down and said, "Quit running from me. I've called you to preach my word." God then gave him the scripture Jeremiah 1:5 (NIV), *"Before I formed you in the womb I knew you, before you were born I set you apart; I appointed you as a prophet to the nations."*

That night Seth surrendered to the call of God on his life. We were thrilled for him to walk into this new season and bought him a Bible in honor of his call. His dad wrote on the inside back cover the prophetic words that are now part of Seth's tattoo testimony: *Percussus Resurgo*, Latin for, "When struck down, I will rise again."

Fast forward to one year after Seth came home from the hospital. I was reading Jeremiah 1:5 to him and felt impressed to read the rest of that chapter. And there it was, in the next verse, another kiss from heaven:

> *"Alas, Sovereign Lord," I said, "**I do not know how to speak**; I am too young." But the Lord said to me, "Do not say, 'I am too young.' You must go to everyone I send you to and say*

whatever I command you. Do not be afraid of them, for I am with you and will rescue you," declares the Lord. **Then the Lord reached out his hand and touched my mouth and said to me, "I have put my words in your mouth."**

— Jeremiah 1:6-9 (NIV)

Besides momentarily uttering the phrase, "Oh, God!" Seth, at this point in his journey (over two years since the encounter with God at Jekyll Island), was still not speaking. Yet, I revisited the past experience in my heart, and though I didn't know how God would pull it off, I believed Seth would speak again. God is into the details and often has plans we could never have imagined. His ways are not our ways. We are not God. And doctors, as intelligent and trained as they are, cannot predict what God will do. So, though we were told that Seth would never speak, I held onto hope that he would preach and testify for the Lord in the future. After all, God had told Seth He wanted him to do it, so I watched and waited.

Chapter 8

HOMEWARD BOUND

*"Love begins at home, and it's not how much we do...but
how much love we put in that action."*

— Mother Teresa

We had been given little hope on September 28, 2011, and for many days to follow, that Seth would survive, but he did. *He did!* We continued to marvel that he had come back from death twice at the scene of his accident and another time after an error was made in the hospital that threatened to take his life. Now here he was, living, breathing, and progressing. We were so relieved and grateful. Five months in the hospital seemed like an eternity in many ways, but finally, the time had come for Seth to be released. It was a couple of days before his 18th birthday.

However, we were bringing home a different Seth to love. I would have moments when I would see glimpses of the "old" Seth, but then they would disappear. I constantly searched for the familiar person I knew and missed. Sometimes he would make some headway in that direction, and a small part of him from the past would emerge and greet me. For instance, I'd recognize a look or a smirk and know that he was tracking with me or with what was happening around him. These were such celebratory moments! Still, I couldn't force him to be the Seth I loved and knew before the accident. I had to accept who he had become and was becoming. In many ways, I had lost a son and now had a new son. I had to get to know *that* Seth and fully accept him as he was.

By the time he was discharged, he was primarily using simple sign language to communicate with us. My sister had taught him to sign "yes" and "no," and we learned to ask him yes and no questions so he could answer us quickly. (He could also sign the words, "I love you.") He suffered from Broca's aphasia[1] and apraxia[2], so he couldn't communicate verbally; he couldn't form words with his mouth. When we spoke to him, he often stared at our lips, studying them to see how we were forming words.

Knowing that his hospital stay was coming to a close, we were more than ready to get him home and start—or restart—our life again with this new version of Seth. But as excited as we were to leave the hospital, a heavy weight of reality was attached. When we wheeled him out the hospital doors and up

---

1   Broca's aphasia is also known as non-fluent and expressive aphasia. The person knows what they want to say but is unable to produce the words or sentence. Broca's aphasia is due to damage to Broca's area in the left hemisphere of the brain, named after French scientist Paul Broca. It is often described as having the words "on the tip of your tongue." It is called non- fluent aphasia because speech is effortful and involves starts and stops. Another defining feature is that if sentences are produced, they often have incorrect syntax, or word order and grammar. (https://www.aphasia.com/aphasia-resource-library/aphasia-types/brocas/)

2   Apraxia is a neurological disorder that affects the brain pathways involved in planning the sequence of movements involved in producing speech. The brain knows what it wants to say, but cannot properly plan and sequence the required speech sound movements. (https:// www.nidcd.nih.gov/health/apraxia-speech)

to our SUV, we would be his primary caregivers. It was a scary thought. Before we left the hospital, we said our goodbyes to the dear nurses, doctors, and therapists with whom we loved and had built strong relationships. There were tears, hugs, and pictures taken, but we kept the fanfare at a minimum so as not to overwhelm Seth. Only his dad and I would be in the car, driving him for what would typically be a four-and-a-half-hour journey home.

We strategically loaded him into the SUV and onto the passenger captain seat, which I had covered with a large towel. We had a five-gallon bucket close at hand, along with waterproof pads to lay over him. I took my place in the back seat captain's chair next to Seth, armed and ready with a backpack full of all the medications, diapers, wipes, food, and other paraphernalia he would need on our journey home. What a trip it turned out to be!

Not long into our ride home, we discovered that driving gave him extreme nausea. Every bump in the road (and there are plenty from New Orleans to our house) made things worse. His dad was as careful as he could be, but Seth would groan each time we hit a bump. Besides the groans, he couldn't articulate when he was about to vomit, so I had to keep looking at his face to know when I needed to get ready with the bucket. As you can imagine, the smell of vomit in the SUV was overpowering. We pulled over when I needed to change Seth, empty the bucket, or give his stomach a moment to settle. Most of the meds required that he take them with food, so I'd have to get him to eat something before giving him his medication. Then, of course, he'd throw up all over again, which included the medicine I'd just given him. We learned, after this, to keep peppermint oil on hand each time we traveled to help mask the odor—for his sake and ours.

Something else I would learn in the months ahead was how challenging it would be to clean him up or get him to a toilet when I was alone with him in public. At first, I thought, *I can't bring him into the women's restroom, and I can't go into the men's or send him in alone.* But then I would dismiss those thoughts and do it anyway because I had to! I'd get some strange looks, which I understood, but I had no choice. I would step into a stall with him, equipped with a backpack stuffed with diapers, a change of clothes, and other supplies. I'd help him sit on the toilet, clean him up, re-diaper him, and change his clothes if they were soiled. None of these steps were a small feat, and he was no small child! This scenario repeated itself for months. A private "family" public restroom would have been helpful, but those are not made available nearly enough.

As we drove away from the hospital and toward home, different emotions churned in my gut. I was thankful that we would have Seth in his own room, back under our roof. I was thrilled that hospital life was behind us, but I was scared to death, too. *What was this going to be like on a daily basis? What progress would he make in the days ahead?*

The four-and-a-half-hour trip back home ended up taking us six grueling hours as we had to go slow and make frequent stops for Seth. Our daughters and my mother were there to greet us when we finally arrived at home. We had survived the long, dramatic drive, but it left the three of us emotionally and physically worn out. Seth's dad and Savannah's fiancé helped him over the threshold of our home, and a new chapter of our journey began. Ready or not, here we go.

I didn't have to wonder long what it would be like having Seth at home and dependent on us for almost everything. His needs surfaced immediately, and we couldn't ring for a nurse. For a while, it would take all of us—a village—to care for him. Our home was not outfitted with ramps and wheelchair accessibility. We did not have a trail of handrails that could steady him or an electric wheelchair so he could get around on his own. For the first several months, we had to get into a rhythm of being needed around the clock. The learning curve was steep as we figured out the best way to do certain things to help Seth. We also had to build up stamina for the constant tasks that needed to be done and the change in the routine of our home and our lives.

For a while, at least one of us slept with him through the night. The first night Seth slept in his bed, his sisters had night duty and slept on either side of him to make sure he didn't roll off the bed or try and get up in the middle of the night. Later, when we felt he was safe enough to sleep alone, we stuck a wireless doorbell near his bed (and another one near the toilet), so he could ring for us to come get him or bring whatever he needed day or night.

We bought many sets of sheets as we had to change them several times a day because the diapers he had to wear couldn't contain everything. I literally wore out both a washer and a dryer with all the laundry that had to be done! It wasn't long before we pulled our backs out with all the lifting, bathing, and changing of sheets, clothes, and diapers, but there was no bell for us to ring for someone to take care of things for us! Besides, we signed up for this. Seth's dad and I wanted to care for our son, and the girls wanted to help their brother, but it was a constant challenge. (It's one thing to know that in your head, and it's another thing to live it out.)

We had to get into the mindset to do just the next thing and to keep moving forward, one task and one need at a time. It wasn't long, however, before we became physically and mentally exhausted and began to suffer emotionally. We were feeling burned out, which is a dangerous place to be. We were still careful not to cry in front of Seth, so while we tended to him and his needs, we held it in. But at night, when he was settled and the day was over, tears would inevitably come—so much so it seemed they would flood the bed. Our family ached from extreme fatigue and deep sadness over what had happened to Seth and how his life would never be the same.

> *I struggled beneath the weight of feeling responsible to "fix it" while knowing I was powerless to do so.*

The strain we felt from Seth's accident, and his five-month hospital stay had been massive. Now, all the care he required from Seth's dad and I put a profound strain on our marriage and, specifically, on my (ex) husband's mental health. He shined for the first year following Seth's accident, and I couldn't have gone through everything without him. He was an invaluable help. But about a year after Seth returned home, he announced that he could no longer continue to take our son to his doctor appointments or help with anything that would require him to have to enter the doors of a hospital. Going to those places triggered PTSD for him, which left me on my own with Seth's frequent visits. (Scheduling doctors' and therapy appointments was an incredibly time-consuming and recurring task that I continued to fulfill, not to mention all the time I spent on the phone and via email advocating for Seth's needs. More on that later). My underlying resentment for Seth's dad grew with my ever-increasing role as Seth's primary caregiver and sole advocate. I felt completely abandoned left to carry the full weight of responsibilities. I wondered how he could just "check out" and throw even more on me, knowing I couldn't afford to let any of it hit the ground because Seth would be the one to ultimately pay the price.

Seth's dad needed me to encourage him often, but I needed encouragement and support as well. I could only do so much, and it wasn't enough for him. After a while, he began to suffer from psychosis. In a very real sense, I now had two patients in my care, both with enormous needs. He was eventually diagnosed with bipolar schizophrenia and was hospitalized twice that year. Still, God was my constant.

Looking back, I know that the only way I was able to maintain my sanity was by God's grace. Several years later, Seth's dad moved out. I ended up taking him back for about a year and a half, but his mental illness became all-consuming, and eventually, he left for good. All this was like an earthquake beneath the surface that set off a tsunami that no one could stop. No one sees the earthquake as it takes place, but when the tsunami hits, many people are affected. They get pummeled by it. We certainly did. Despite my best efforts, Seth was in a spiral of depression and anger. I struggled beneath the weight of feeling responsible to "fix it" while knowing I was powerless to do so. I would fall into bed and feel smothered by all the emotions and that voice of inadequacy that is all too familiar to caregivers.

Thankfully, God, in His grace and mercy, met me in my battle. He gave me an extra dose of strength, and I was able to push through. He brought some people to me for support. After that tumultuous time, our home would no longer include Seth's dad, but it would continue to be a place of recovery and love.

Chapter 9

CAREGIVER BY DEFAULT

"Talk to yourself like you would to someone you love."

— Brené Brown

Let me just say right now that if you're reading this and you find yourself in the role of caregiver, I want you to know that I understand the demand placed on you to take care of your loved one is exhausting and thankless. The lack of sleep, accompanied by mental exhaustion, can be overwhelming at times. Many people won't understand the weight you are under. Well-meaning friends and family may not offer help because they mistakenly think you have it all together.

Like I did, at first, you probably find yourself mechanically going through the motions of caring for your patient's needs while trying to maintain your day-to-day responsibilities. The phrase "Not enough hours in the day" is your everyday reality, and you wonder how you'll ever catch up with the tasks that keep piling up. You're busy from morning until night! I'm sure you didn't wake up one morning and think, "This is my dream job. I want to be a caregiver." But, here you are, a caregiver by default.

If you're not careful, you'll find yourself unable to move past the tragedy that forever changed your life. You'll find yourself holding on tightly to what was because the fear that you will forget the original version of your loved one is even more terrifying than the painful memories. Do you unconsciously punish yourself by not living your life? Do you think, *How can I move on when he (or she) cannot? How can I enjoy life, or even smile, while life has forever changed for my loved one?* If this is you, recognize what you're doing. Open your eyes to it and be honest with yourself. Don't spend your life in a graveyard full of regret and loss, unable to move past what was lost. You do have a life to live. I promise.

Maybe you didn't lose someone, but rather something. Perhaps it was the life you had or should've had. Part of moving on in a healthy way is doing something to honor the memory of the person or thing you lost. It is especially helpful to do something positive when the difficult anniversary date of your loss comes around.

One of the most beneficial and healing things I did was create the Team Seth Foundation for Traumatic Brain Injury Awareness. This 501c3 non-profit organization gave me a platform to share Seth's story and not only raise money for others but raise awareness for invisible disabilities such as brain injury, apraxia, and aphasia. (As I write this book, it was announced that actor Bruce Willis has been diagnosed with aphasia, though the cause of his acquired aphasia is yet to be disclosed. This condition can develop for several reasons, including brain damage from stroke, aneurysm, blockage or rupture of blood vessels, brain tumor or infection, and seizures. Even migraines can cause it. Many are also born with aphasia. Through Bruce's willingness to go public with his diagnosis, many more people will become more interested and informed.) As a parent of someone with a brain injury, I was able to share my personal experience of how I dealt with the trauma of Seth's injury and guide others on how to navigate through their own. It helped me bring something positive out of my pain. Speaking about how Seth's brain injury impacted our lives helped others not feel so alone as they dealt with their own diagnosis. It made people realize they can also use their pain to encourage others. So, I continue to be outspoken to this day. That's one of the reasons for this book: to let you know that you, too, can find purpose in your pain.

How to Live Again

A first step to living your life, even though it has been radically changed, is not isolating yourself. As a caregiver, it's easy to do because you wind up bearing the weight of responsibility. Strong people make it look easy and look like they don't need any help, but nobody is *that* strong! If you're putting up a façade like this, beware. It is a surefire way to physically collapse.

If you're not very good at asking for help, you will wind up doing it all alone and then resent that no one is helping you. You get what you ask for, and if you don't ask, you don't get. Don't assume people know. Be specific and ask for help with what you need. Then be willing to accept the hands of those reaching out to you.

Be mindful that people who have not experienced this type

of grief will not understand what you're going through. When you voice your frustrations or vent your anger, some may be quick to shame or guilt you with their "at-least-he-didn't-die" comments. Words like these only add to the heavy burden you already bear. Don't take them to heart. They were most likely said out of ignorance and not meant to be cruel. (And even if they were meant to be cruel, discard them from your mind. They're rubbish.)

While caring for your loved one, don't forget to take care of yourself. This may sound trivial in light of what you are experiencing, but one aspect of living again is giving some attention to your appearance. If you're a woman, ditch the yoga pants once in a while for some stylish jeans or a skirt and put on some lipstick. Rock those earrings. Get your nails done. Whatever makes you feel pretty, do that. For you men, it's usually easier. Just take a few minutes to shave and put a comb through your hair. Put on a clean shirt that makes you feel good. As insignificant as this may seem when you consider all that's going on, I promise that spending a little time on yourself will help you feel more normal and boost your confidence. Of course, some days (most days at first), you will be lucky if you can find the time to brush your teeth, but as regularly as possible, give yourself permission to treat yourself. Get a massage or have a spa day. Or get a coffee and go sit in the park. You don't have to spend a lot of money.

In addition to maintaining a little dignity with your appearance, take a short time on a regular basis to do something you enjoy. Spend an hour on your hobby. Lose yourself in a good book. Get outside and feel the sun on your face. Go for a walk or a swim, put on some music and dance–however you enjoy being active–and clear your mind. Engaging in exercise is proven to help alleviate or curb depression. Invest some time in yourself and in meeting your needs. This isn't selfish; it's wise and ultimately will help sustain you as you continue in your role as a caregiver.

Finding a support group for caregivers is another significant thing to help you live again. It is therapeutic and (and also necessary) for your mental well-being to communicate with someone who has been through (or going through) something similar. Many online groups offer an empathetic ear and a safe place to share without fear of harsh judgment. You are not alone in this journey. There is a staggering amount of people in a similar boat as you and your loved one. For example, according to the Centers for Disease Control and Prevention (CDC), an estimated 1.5 million people in the United States alone suffer from a traumatic brain injury each year. (In 2019-2020, this represented more than 611 TBI-related hospitalizations and 176 TBI-related deaths *per day)*. These estimates don't include the many traumatic brain injuries treated only in emergency rooms, primary care, and urgent care facilities.[3] There are also those that go untreated. Do you see? You are not alone. Your loved one, who is a survivor (something to be celebrated), is not alone either.

Traumatic brain injury is life-altering. It changes the person you once knew and loved into someone you no longer recognize. Your injured son, daughter, parent, or husband may

---

3   https://www.cdc.gov/traumaticbraininjury/data/index.html

have the same body and the same face, but they are strangers. Who they were no longer exists. The sooner you come to grips with that fact and accept who they are now, the sooner you can move forward in accepting your new normal. Don't try to force the person they are now into a mold of who they once were. By doing so, you unintentionally send the message that the "new version" of them is not acceptable. Remember, Seth lost many pre-injury memories, and when we talked about his past, he said it was like hearing about a stranger. Sharing stories about your loved one pre-injury can be very upsetting for them. For all intents and purposes, that life is lost.

> *If you don't grieve what was and accept what is, you will remain stuck in emotional purgatory.*

This is why it is so important to allow yourself to grieve. I believe it's easier to permit yourself to do that when that person has physically died. It's very different when the person's body is still present, but the person you knew no longer exists. How do you grieve the loss of someone who is still alive?

I've devoted an entire chapter to help you navigate the stages of grief, but for now, I want to impress upon you that you're not doing anything wrong. You can't fix normal, and grieving is a normal part of loss. You cannot avoid it. You must go *through* it. Staying in grief is like getting in a boat and letting the current take you where it wants. You will wander aimlessly, with no purpose or reason to live. An important part of living again is grieving well. (Everyone grieves differently, so be careful not to compare yourself with anyone else.)

There will be days when you feel like you have finally moved on, while other days will feel as if you're back at square one. You know you need to move forward but don't know how. If you don't grieve what was and accept what is, you will remain stuck in emotional purgatory. The choice is yours. You can grieve but then get up, wash your face, and live, knowing and believing you still have a purpose. Or, you can make the opposite choice and resolve to stay in a state of constant grief. You can choose to throw in the towel, but how will that help you or anyone else? It will be challenging at first, but the more you talk about it, the easier it becomes to make the best choice and keep doing the next right thing. And keep in mind, there is someone desperate for the hope you have to give. Open your eyes and heart to those in your sphere of influence. When you reach out, you will be blessed and become a blessing to them.

And remember, you don't have to go through this process alone. Ask for help!

Don't Fight Alone

There is comfort in knowing you are not fighting alone. I was so grateful for my friends, family, and church family, who fought alongside me and prayed for my son. We called them the Team Seth Prayer Warriors. They interceded with specific, focused prayers. Every time we received a bad report, an S.O.S. prayer request went out by group text and via Facebook to the Team

Seth Prayer Warriors. Many continue to pray for Seth and our family to this day.

I don't know where you stand when it comes to your faith and belonging to a church, but I can't express strongly enough how important and helpful it is. I encourage you to connect with a local church that believes in the power of prayer and exercises that belief. When you are in a crisis, prayer is essential. (If you don't have faith, you can pray and ask God to help you have it! He wants to give it to you.) Knowing that Seth was in the fight of his life (and I was, too, in my own way) compelled me to rally the troops on a regular basis and ask for prayer. No matter your situation as you read this, remember that the battlefield is no place to collapse. You need a group of people that can hold you up in prayer when you are too weary to stand.

In addition to always being ready to take to their knees for us, many dedicated prayer warriors also helped meet some of our practical needs. As I mentioned, my mom came regularly to help with Seth and clean my house for me. I needed breaks to shower and catch my breath. I also needed to know that Seth was being looked after when I had to spend time making calls or writing emails on his behalf. I had no time or energy to mop, vacuum, do dishes, clean bathrooms, or anything else related to the house during those first few months of Seth being home. My mom gave me a tremendous gift by taking on this task. Some of our neighbors and church family cooked meals and delivered them to us. One woman ordered several ready-made, frozen casserole dishes from a nice restaurant and brought them over. Her thoughtfulness and generosity touched me, especially since we barely knew each other. People often initiated helping in some way, but I also had to learn how to ask for help when needed.

Whatever you are struggling with today, reach out to someone. It's okay to not be okay. Don't let the enemy's lies convince you that you have to keep your needs and struggles hidden. Don't let the devil convince you that others won't understand or that you will be an imposition. Ask for prayer support. Let people know of your practical needs. That being said, be aware that help often is for a season. Most people want to do something to assist you when they realize there is a need, but after a while, they go back to their own lives and routines. Accept the help when it comes, but know some of it (much of it) will be temporary. This reality was hurtful to me for a while. I've felt abandoned in this journey from time to time, but I also recognize and am thankful for the help I have received. I still have to ask for help from time to time. There is no shame in that.

Everyone struggles at some point, but it is dangerous to struggle in silence. There are people who care about you and want to be there for you. They will fight with you, but you have to say something. Don't fight alone, or you will die alone.

Chapter 10

SETH ON THE MOVE

"With God's help we will do mighty things...."

— Psalm 108:13 (NLT)

As difficult as it was to be a full-time caregiver to someone with so many needs (especially in those first few months when I was learning the ropes), I knew that Seth's battle was even bigger. My compassion and empathy for him were off the charts and had been since the moment I learned of his brain injury. He was in constant pain. His headaches were chronic and other areas of his body ached, which killed me as a mother. But despite the pain, we slowly began seeing a shift in his progress when Seth returned home. At the hospital, we'd been told that most of his recovery—if it would happen at all—would occur at home. Seth had a drive in him that was impressive, to say the least, and that drive kicked in even more under our roof.

Seth's dad wanted to get him up and moving as soon as possible after he returned home, which was wise, but it took a couple of months before we could see that Seth was ready for the challenge. We knew that part of our role as caregivers was to actively push Seth toward recovery, but we also recognized it was a huge transition for him to be at home. He had to get used to and figure out his new surroundings, and for someone with a brain injury, change is especially exhausting. One of the most common realities for a brain injury survivor is neuro-fatigue. Even today, when Seth has a lot of "newness" going on, it affects him mentally and physically. He seems to regress when he experiences neuro-fatigue, but the truth is his brain just needs to rest. His brain has to work harder than before his accident to process things. So, tasks that required concentration, including adjusting to and navigating a new environment like he had to do when he returned home, are a wipe-out for Seth. Add physical effort to that, and the fatigue is debilitating. Neuro-fatigue can also promote depression, so we were careful to stay in tune with Seth's energy level and not overtax him or push him too soon.

When the day came that we felt Seth was strong enough and ready for the challenge, his dad and brother-in-law got on either side of him and began walking him up and down our driveway. This would have been difficult for Seth had the driveway been flat, but it had a steep slope to it, which anyone with well-working legs griped about when they had to make the trek! For Seth, it must have felt like he was climbing a mountain. Yet, he kept on. With a determined look on his face, he walked it with their help. Despite the pain, he pushed through it.

This was the Seth I knew. It was bittersweet when I would catch glimpses of him off and on. I had seen it months earlier as he exhibited determination and his "can-do" spirit in the hospital when they first got him out of bed and put him on his feet, holding him as he stood. Sometimes, while struggling to progress, Seth would grow frustrated, and I would feel bad for him. But Lori (the kind-hearted but drill-sergeant-like physical therapist that worked with him in the hospital) shed some light on this, and her words have stayed with me. She said it was a good thing when Seth would get frustrated because it meant he was all in. If he wasn't frustrated, it would mean he didn't care and wasn't trying. So actually, in this case, his frustration was a positive sign! He was taking the next step (literally and figuratively) toward recovery and more independence as he walked up and down our driveway using his dad and brother-in-law as human crutches. As I watched him, I had to remember to breathe. I was so nervous!

Due to the left-side brain damage he sustained in the accident, Seth was hemi-paralyzed on the right side of his body. I had a legitimate reason to fear that he would fall and hurt himself while relearning to walk. I had to keep in mind another thing that Lori told me when I had these initial concerns: "Falling down is an important part of learning to walk because it teaches you how to get back up again." (Lori also taught Seth how to roll over and sit up if he ever fell—a practical thing to learn.) The average person walks thirty feet on their first day trying after such a debilitating injury. On November 15, 2011, Seth took his first step (with assistance) in the hospital. Not only did he take his first step that day (wearing the same shoes he was wearing during the accident, no less), but Seth also pushed past the fear of falling and walked 187 feet!

Remembering all he had accomplished in the hospital brought tears to my eyes as I now stood in front of our house watching Seth move forward to tackle the next-level challenge. He was making strides. He may have come home in a wheelchair, but I was hopeful that we could get rid of that thing

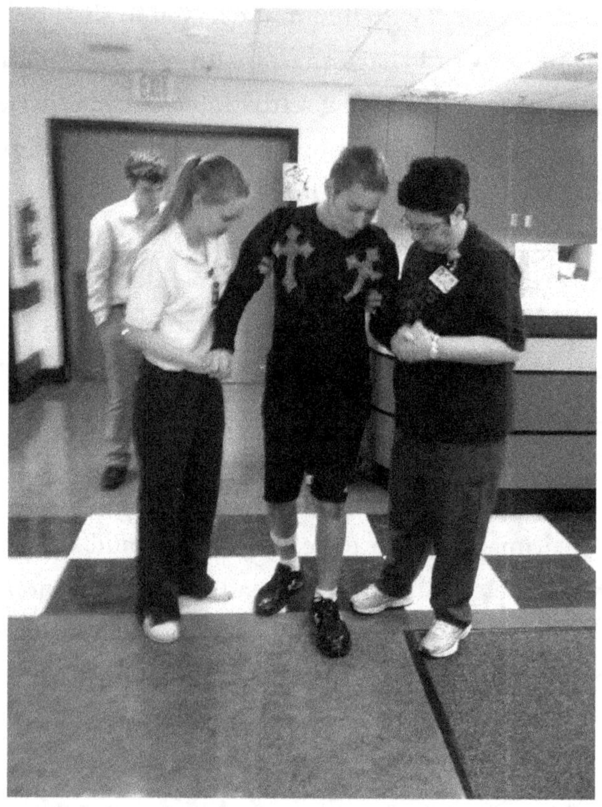

Seth relearning to walk in New Orleans Children's Hospital

before too long, even if it meant him taking a fall from time to time. Seeing him walking on our sloped driveway, even with assistance, was cause for celebration. Still, I found myself living in fear quite a bit. I would take that fear to the furthest level and visualize, not only Seth falling but injuring himself beyond repair. I had to fight these fears and resist the urge to go there in my mind so they wouldn't be allowed to swallow me up. Fear, if not managed, is paralyzing.

And hopelessness will rob you of life. Fear and despair need to be kicked to the curb in order to move forward. No matter what you are going through, I encourage you to do yourself a favor and make the most of this day God has given you. You may be struggling physically or emotionally. Perhaps you are recovering from a traumatic brain injury, fighting a dreadful diagnosis, or you are a full-time caregiver feeling discouraged and exhausted. Whatever your circumstances are, face the day with hope. Call out fear, and don't focus on it. Instead, summon the courage to live out what comes your way, and you may be pleasantly surprised. How you will do this will take some thought and some determination. Do your best to not waste a single breath and take the time to recognize the good things. Celebrate them. Speak positive words, even if you feel like cursing. You have the power to control your attitude about any situation—both good and bad. No matter how impossible it may appear or how bad you feel about it, you have the power to change your perception, so be careful not to give your power away. Don't go by how you feel. Emotions will lie to you. Fear will squash you. Take charge, and speak to your tomorrow, your next week, or even your next year. You will see that feelings of hopelessness will disappear.

How many times in the past have you gone through something that you thought would kill you? Or thought you would lose your mind? Yet, here you are, alive and still breathing. You are here on purpose! When you share what you've gone through with someone who is struggling, you give purpose to your pain. So, speak up about it.

Also, stop living in the shadow of your past failures. It's not a failure if you learn from it! It is simply a part of the process of success. Don't blame the past, your ex, or your financial situation another day for your unhappiness. Every time you fall and get back up again, you are one step closer to your goal. Setbacks aren't really setbacks—they're simply part of the comeback.

These truths were lived out for me as I watched my son push through his pain and fatigue and move forward. He survived the barrage of setbacks in the hospital, and (spoiler alert!), he would experience many more in the days to come, but he kept on. As much as I wanted to inspire him each day, he inspired me. Step by step, Seth was making progress on his comeback. But that's not to say he progressed every day. That's not the way it works with traumatic brain injuries. It's not a slow journey where you gradually get better each day. Seth was on the move, that's true, but comebacks are rarely, if ever, linear. They go up and down and sideways. There are so many twists and turns to recovery; it's staggering and keeps you on your toes. Pushing on emotionally, mentally, physically, and spiritually must remain your stance to move forward and progress.

Pushing Past Limitations

As I mentioned, Seth always loved to be challenged. He even talked about joining the armed forces to identify his limitations and prove to himself he could overcome them. He was especially intrigued by the process it took to become a Navy SEAL. There's a defining week in SEAL training called Hell Week.

Hell Week is a brutal seven days designed to test physical and mental endurance under extreme stress and sleep deprivation.

Above all, it tests determination and desire. On average, only 25% of SEAL candidates make it through Hell Week. It is often the greatest achievement of their lives, and with it comes the realization that they can do more than they ever thought possible. Those that succeed are not necessarily the largest or strongest men but those who desire it most—those who push through the pain.

While he was in the early days of his hospital stay, following another shunt revision surgery that brought with it more complications, I reminded Seth about Hell Week:

"Remember, those who want to be part of the elite SEAL team are pushed to see where their breaking point is. Pushing past the pain and their limitations is a crucial part of proving they have what it takes. I know you have what it takes, son. Now, show them what you're made of. Show them you are a warrior! The devil couldn't destroy your body, so he's trying to destroy your mind. I need you to speak positive things to yourself as you've always done, Seffer!"

— Kimber Hanchey, November 4, 2011

If you're caring for someone who is fighting for recovery, remember this: The one thing you can't give a person is the "want to." The desire has to come from within them. You can speak motivational words of encouragement. You can pray for them. Both of these things are significant and helpful. But, their burning desire, their fight for recovery, is up to them. Therapists and doctors can give them all the tools, but it's up to them to apply them. It takes *pushing through it,* especially on the days when they don't feel like it or want to. It takes a *there-ain't-no-quit-in-me* attitude of determination and perseverance. Seth had, and still has, times of great discouragement and weariness with all the work that recovery requires, but his determination to push through it triumphed. From there, victories, big and small, came. They are his victories that I am privileged

> You will never know if you have the courage to defeat a giant until you stand face-to-face with one.

to share. (Remember, don't ignore the "small" victories. They matter. Acknowledge them. Celebrate them.) As a caregiver, I have enjoyed victories over the years, too. You don't have to be a SEAL to experience this! Pushing past limitations brings rewards to all of us.

Your Stopping Point Is Where You Say It Is

As I've shown you through our story so far, the road to recovery is not an easy one. If you're reading this and dealing with an injury or difficult diagnosis, you will have to push through pain and weariness on days you feel like it would be easier to just give up. The amount of fight you put into it is up to you. I learned that within weeks of spending time with Seth in the hospital. I had a front-row seat as I daily observed his fight.

It's never easy to push through something painful, especially when faced with a seemingly impossible situation. You may feel like giving up. You may even have legitimate reasons to quit. At the end of the day, how far you go in life depends on how bad you want it. And no one else can want it for you. The good news is that you have everything inside of you that you need to succeed. Remember, you have your Father's DNA. No, I'm not talking about the man your mother slept with. You were created with the stuff champions are made of by a Creator who loves you.

The difference between winners and losers is where they decide to quit. No one can tell you where that is. The decision is yours. Those who keep going and cross the finish line are the ones who take the prize. You may not come in first place, but you're still a winner if you cross the finish line. Don't quit now! Face another day. Do what you can with what you have in you.

I continue to draw strength for myself by reading Scripture and often share it with Seth. Take in what King David wrote in this Psalm and think about how God made you and what that means for you today:

I thank you, God, for making me so mysteriously complex! Everything you do is marvelously breathtaking. It simply amazes me to think about it! How thoroughly you know me, Lord. You even formed every bone in my body when you created me in the secret place; carefully, skillfully you shaped me from nothing to something. You saw who you created me to be before I became me! Before I'd ever seen the light of day, the number of days you planned for me were already recorded in your book.

— Psalm 139:14-16 (TPT)

Your Comeback Will Be Greater Than Your Setback

You will never know if you have the courage to defeat a giant until you stand face-to-face with one. It's not until you are staring at an intimidating obstacle that appears impossible to overcome that you realize you have the strength within you to defeat it. The will to win cannot be measured by anything on the outside. It's the fight to come back that's on the inside that determines how far you go. You don't learn what your capacity is until you are forced to carry that weight.

I can't give you too many details of those days during that first year back home with Seth. First of all, so much of it is a blur to me. (I'm the type of person who thrives on being busy, but those days were ridiculous!) But, I can tell you the setbacks continued. And then some comebacks would take place. Up and down. On and on. Around and around. Setback, comeback, setback, comeback…It's a dance or, perhaps more accurately, a rollercoaster that requires steadfastness, determination, and support. Seth had all those things and more. And, through it all, God was there.

Chapter 11

"ALL GOD"

— Helen H. Lemmel (from the chorus of
Turn Your Eyes Upon Jesus)

Seth's language center was completely destroyed after the accident. As a result of his traumatic brain injury, he acquired Broca's aphasia and apraxia, both of which affected his communication and speech. When he was discharged from the hospital, he could only say three "words": *yah, ma,* and *nah.* He soon learned two more words: *All God.* That simple phrase became a constant reminder of where his help came from and where all glory should go. To this day, whenever he encourages someone facing an impossible situation, he points his finger toward heaven and says, "All God." Seth knows that He is the factor that changes every outcome.

What do you do when you're faced with a setback? With every obstacle and every setback, I watched Seth fight to push through and focus on the next step. It took discipline and a conscious effort for him to not get stuck in despair.

I vividly remember one instance a little over a month after the accident. Seth had a lot of fluid on his brain and was scheduled for yet another surgery to put in a drain tube. That morning started out (as so many did back then) with a bad report about the severity of his brain damage and the familiar litany of all the things he would never be able to do. We were constantly told he would never be able to comprehend a sentence, much less a joke, and that he wouldn't have any memories of who he was or who we were to him.

We fought hard to flip the script and stay focused on the positive. On the day of that particular surgery, we posted something on Facebook. Here is an excerpt:

Seth will be going to surgery today to have a drain tube put into the right side of his brain. They're trying to alleviate accumulation of the fluid. There's quite a lot, and this is causing more pressure on the brain. Pray this will be successful. They will not remove his trachea until they are sure the swelling is under control. He has made a lot of progress, but there is so much more to go! This is still a large and steep mountain to climb, but we will not give up, and neither will my strong son. Fight hard, Team Seth, in prayer.

— Kimber Hanchey October 22, 2011

My oldest daughter, Savannah, called that same day and said, *"Mom, the devil tried to take Seth's life and couldn't. He struck him in a place that would take his gift, but he can't take Seth's gift because it belongs to God. So don't let him fool you with how it looks. God's going to restore Seth completely!!!"*

We were hit with many storms—some more destructive than others. We learned that praising God in the storm changed things. While it did not change our situation, it shifted our focus back to God. He will do the same for you and speak *peace* in the midst of your storm. Though the storm may continue to rage *around* you, it will no longer rage *inside* of you. God will quiet the howling winds and still the raging seas as you keep your eyes on Him. I can testify to this as it has been my experience and Seth's experience over and over again.

> Though the storm may continue to rage **around** you, it will no longer rage **inside** of you. God will quiet the howling winds and still the raging seas as you keep your eyes on Him.

A weekly scene from our life that began when Seth returned home took place at church. He wanted to attend Sunday services, and we were dedicated to making it happen for him. It was no small task. To arrive at church on time, we would have to get Seth out of bed early on Sunday so he could bathe. Again, we didn't have a handicap-accessible shower for him (anything that converts an area to be handicap accessible is very expensive). Seth's dad would put on his swim trunks and take Seth into the stall to help him get clean. Once he was bathed, we'd diaper him with two diapers—one wrapped around his "parts" and the other used the usual way. (This was a trick that I even showed his nurses. Wearing just one diaper never worked successfully.) Then, because it was important to Seth to look nice, we'd dress him in a suit and bring an extra one in the car just in case he soiled the one he was wearing.

After the two-hour ordeal of getting him ready, we'd load him into the SUV and drive the 40 miles to church, stopping when we needed to empty his vomit bucket or change his diaper. Once we made it to church, we would settle him into the office, where he would sit and wait for us to get things ready for the service. Then, Danny, one of our congregants (a big dude with an even bigger heart and some strong muscle), would bring Seth to the sanctuary and take him to where he insisted on sitting–in the front row. Seth refused to use his arm brace, leg brace, or wheelchair at church, nor would he take a seat during our worship time. So, Danny would hold him up for the 20-30 minutes. During this time, Seth would raise his left hand in praise to God, his right hand still clenched in a fist at his side, unable to open. There was radiant joy on his face! It was beautiful. Here was this kid, living in pain, unable to stand on his own, wearing diapers, and still praising God with all he had. As people took in this sight, I'm sure it put their troubles into perspective. Seth trusted God wholeheartedly despite the severe storm of life he was in. We are all wise to take that to heart and offer thankfulness and praise no matter what we're experiencing. It can only happen when we keep our focus on God.

A few years ago, I took a motorcycle driving course. The instructor warned us about target fixation, which means the motorcycle will go wherever your eyes are looking. Many riders wreck because they are focused on a pothole in the road and tend to ride straight into it. The instructor advised us to look

Seth (after he regained some use of his right arm)
holding the arm and leg braces and standing next to
the wheelchair he was supposed to be confined to.

past an obstacle instead of focusing on what we wanted to avoid. When you do so, your mind steers you around it.

When you're in the midst of a storm, look into your heavenly Father's eyes. Focus on Him instead of the insurmountable obstacle you're facing. He will guide you through what would otherwise take you down. Then, you can point upward and declare with joy on your face, "All God!"

Chapter 12

RUN FOR IT!

"He gives strength to the weary and increases the power of the weak. Even youths grow tired and weary, and young men stumble and fall; but those who hope in the Lord will renew their strength...they will run and not grow weary, they will walk and not be faint."

— Isaiah 40:29-31 (NIV)

For quite a while, Seth continued to walk up and down our driveway, with his dad holding one arm and his brother-in-law holding the other. His balance was horrendous at first, and they served as human crutches for him. I know there were times Seth didn't feel like getting outside and putting forth the effort. As he walked he would cry, but he kept going. He kept practicing, and each time he would walk a little longer and a little further. Day by day, he was getting stronger. We could see it, and I believe he could feel it. Then one day, he pushed his human crutches away and started walking on his own! At that moment, the words, "He'll never walk again," echoed in my mind. I had heard that statement many times from the doctors at the hospital, but I held on to hope that they weren't true. Now, in front of our house, Seth was proving the doctors wrong just months after he left the hospital. God was doing a great work, and this was only the beginning.

Going from walking while being assisted to walking on his own was a miracle, but God and Seth took it further, and it wasn't long after walking on his own that he started jogging and then running! It was a miraculous sight! All God. As he experienced these milestones, Seth's face beamed. He laughed. I'm sure he was laughing out of the sheer pleasure of the accomplishment, but it was more profound than that. He must have felt a renewed sense of freedom. Think about it: Since his accident, he had been constantly surrounded by medical staff and family members. While in the hospital, someone was next to him 24/7 to ensure he wasn't in danger and provide for his needs. He had to be assisted with almost every task for nearly a year. Now, while outside with the sun on his face, he was moving–literally making strides–on his own. Sheer joy!

Moments of Impact

I would have never imagined that my son would have to learn to walk all over again (after learning to walk as a toddler so many years before), but life is fragile and has a way of humbling us. There are Moments of Impact in life that can leave us questioning if we'll be able to live through them. It is in times like these that our true character is revealed. It's no longer about living our life to impress others or even gaining their approval; it's about the fight to survive. Can you relate?

If Seth had given up the fight, no amount of us prodding

him to keep on, to put forth the effort, to push past the pain would have amounted to much. Seth had to be willing to fight on, not only to survive but to have a chance at experiencing victories. His will to push through the seemingly insurmountable challenges revealed (and continues to reveal) Seth's character. My role as caregiver was to be his cheerleader and remind him of the qualities God had infused into him before he was even born. *"Son, there is greatness in you." "Seth, you are strong." "You are fighter."* He had the eye of the tiger before his accident, and that determination was still in him after the accident, maybe more so. Seth's accident was a Moment of Impact from which he had to recover and overcome. Many would have wallowed in despair

> *There are Moments of Impact in life that can leave us questioning if we'll be able to live through them. It is in times like these that our true character is revealed.*

feeling sorry for themselves (or given up altogether) because of the lot life had thrown at them. Not Seth. But that isn't to say that he didn't have hard days (that would sometimes turn into hard weeks). He definitely did and still does, but he refused to let them define him and take over. He pushed *through* them.

What happens as a result of those Moments of Impact can be pretty amazing, and it not only applies to Seth, but I believe it applies to you. Once you make up your mind to overcome, you will impress yourself with your resolve to stand and fight. You will see strength revealed that you would have otherwise never known existed. You will find out what you're truly made of, whether you are the survivor or the caregiver. *Some would have thrown in the towel by now, but not you.*

The fact that you are reading this is proof that you haven't given up the fight. I believe nothing is by chance. God is far too big for chance. He is a God of divine appointment. Let this be the sign you need. He sees you. He hears you. He's got you. And you will overcome it.

Team Seth

One thing that helped me overcome, as my heart broke for my son, was taking on some challenges for myself. I was still mourning what was and what would never be our "normal" again. But these challenges helped to give me the upper hand in my fight to stay healthy emotionally, mentally, and physically. It's not that I had leisure time that needed to be filled! I continued to stay very busy taking care of Seth. This included scheduling his doctor's appointments and taking him to each one. I spent a lot of time reaching out to agencies and nonprofit groups who may be able to provide financial assistance and practical equipment to help Seth and so much more. One way I felt I could move toward healing was to throw myself into turning the tide on this disaster in our lives. I knew we could do this by helping others.

My motivation for starting the Team Seth Foundation for Traumatic Brain Injury Awareness was to encourage others who were going through what we were experiencing. I also wanted the organization to provide financial assistance to children diagnosed with traumatic brain injury. I couldn't have imagined at the time, however, how we would end up being a help to countless people dealing with a variety of challenges from all over the world! It has been mind-blowing and another example of "All God!"

As the organization was just beginning, we held a 5K race to bring awareness and raise funds. The first race was held near our home on Seth's 19th birthday at Lincoln Parish Park on March 1, 2013. The most impressive part of that race was that Seth ran it! Just one year after coming home from the hospital in a wheelchair, he ran the entire thing and publicly proved everyone wrong who ever thought "never" would be his reality.

In the days that followed, Seth not only continued to walk, jog, and run on his own, but he even rode his (repaired) bike—the same bike he rode the day of his accident. As he moved forward in his recovery and was able to do more, I realized we needed to keep resetting the bar. He needed a new challenge. Knowing that Seth is goal-driven by nature, we set some goals for him to aim for and gave him a vision for accomplishing them so his progress wouldn't peak sooner than needed. Even though he had never engaged in weightlifting before his accident, I suggested he try it. It seemed like a wise next step, so my son-in-law began taking him to the gym. The two of them would spend a couple of hours there several times a week. They took it slow at first. Seth was still living with hemiparesis on his right side, so I had my son-in-law start him out on the machines because it seemed like the safest way to begin. He started by doing forward leg curls without any weights, but it wasn't long before weights were added, and Seth maxed out that machine! From

Seth crossing the finish line at the first
Team Seth Foundation 5k, March 1, 2013

there, he worked out his arms on the butterfly machine, and, you guessed it, he maxed out those weights too! Our theory was if his brain could believe that he was strong enough, he could make his body do it. Seth still thought that his right side was his dominant side although that wasn't reality. To this day, he has not regained full strength on that side, yet his brain says, "your right side is able," and so it is!

I continued thinking outside the box regarding Seth's recovery. When I saw the physical strength he possessed and how much he enjoyed lifting, I began making calls to see how I could help him progress and flourish to his fullest potential. I ended up walking into a gym near our home and sharing Seth's story. This is how I started every conversation as I advocated for him, and then I'd say, "Please help me help my son." There was an experienced trainer there that day named Tommy, and he not only listened to what I had to say, but he heard the need. This was another kiss from heaven. Tommy agreed to work with Seth and kept him busy with different types of lifting. He had Seth flipping giant tires and doing a variety of strength-building exercises. Seth loved his time in the gym, but some days, when he was especially hurting, it took a lot for him to go.

On top of that, his neuro-fatigue would hit him hard. Lifting in different sections of the gym was a challenge because he had to navigate new equipment and learn new tasks. To train well, you need to confuse your muscles, so you don't do the same things over and over and plateau. New exercises and new lifts were regularly introduced into Seth's workout. This was good for his muscles but taxing on his brain. It exhausted him to learn new things, and we had to be mindful of that as he worked out.

Through the training process, Tommy was aware that Seth needed to keep setting goals. He suggested that they run in the Hotter Than Hell Marathon. Seth accepted the challenge, ran it, and continued meeting every new challenge Tommy would set. Finally, he said Seth should try powerlifting and suggested that I look into having him compete in the Special Olympics. I knew nothing about the Special Olympics then, but I would soon become somewhat of an expert! My philosophy when it came to anything that might be a help to Seth was, "You tell me what to do and point me in the direction, and I will run like a madwoman to make whatever needs to happen, happen! What I don't know, I will figure out!" Google was my friend, and I was never shy about calling people and asking them for information or soliciting their help. My motivation was Seth and igniting purpose out of the pain. I was fired up to do all I could to help my son, and God supplied me with the energy, focus, and contacts I needed to make things happen.

I called the Louisiana State office, told them where I lived and that I wanted to find out about getting my son into the Special Olympics. I was told that the gentleman overseeing events in our area had died several years before from cancer, and no one had stepped in to take his place. In fact, I discovered that no one was involved in organizing *anything* in our area for this movement. "Well, I'll do it," I heard myself say, and just like that, I was in and passionately involved!

I took the reins and moved forward with my journey with the Special Olympics by first heading to Louisiana Tech University to meet with someone there who could be a resource. I pitched Seth's story and convinced them to allow me to host a powerlifting meet for the Special Olympics on campus. I knew nothing about powerlifting at the time. Still, I managed to get a trainer from South Louisiana to host an event for anyone interested in competing in powerlifting with the Special Olympics. From there, I discovered that no one was overseeing other parishes in our area—thirteen in all! I felt compelled to take them on as well. "I'll do it!" became my mantra. And I quickly found out that "I'll do it" meant a huge undertaking!

My team of volunteers and I hosted a Field Day for the kids who wanted to compete. Close to a thousand people showed up at our Northeast meet held at ULM. It was the largest gathering of this kind that had ever taken place in that area for the Special Olympics. It was a beautiful day in every way. A director of the Special Olympics attended our event. As the competitions were in full swing, he came out onto the field to talk to me. "I know you're busy," he said, "and you're running around doing so much, but I want to show you something." He then had me follow him up the stands. He told me to look down at the field below when we reached the top. "I want you to look at what you did today." From that vantage point, I was able to take in all the different events I had organized and see the athletes in action. It brought tears to my eyes to see all those special-needs kids playing and having fun on the field. I praised God for what we were able to accomplish that day—not only for Seth but for so many others. It was a privilege to be a part of something so (pardon the pun) *special*!

From there, Seth started competing and powerlifting at other venues, and it was a scene I had to soak in. Here was this young man who had never lifted weights before in his life, and he was a legitimate contender. He was still numb in his right-side extremities, but he was breaking records! Opportunities began to open up for him.

I heard about a gym in our area that I thought might be able to help Seth get to the next level, so I paid them a visit. As I entered the gym, I shared Seth's story, as was my routine, and then boldly asked, "Is there anybody here who can help train my son?" The woman I spoke with listened intently to what I was telling her. I could tell she was moved by it. She then asked me to wait while she ran and got her husband, Rupert. It turned out that he owned the gym and had previously participated in the Olympics as a powerlifter for Britain. Both he and his wife became emotional as the three of us talked, and they learned more about Seth's story. Finally, Rupert said, "I'd like to train your son and help him take home the gold." God had led me to the right place!

With his new coach's help, Seth ended up representing the Louisiana Delegation in the 2018 Special Olympics USA Games. It was only the fifth time he had competed in power-lifting in his life! (And even then, it was only at state and local competitions.) Going into the games, his coach estimated that he would squat 400 pounds, bench press 315 pounds, and dead-lift 450 pounds, and Seth came close to that prediction. Seth won medals in every event he competed in during the games. He won a bronze medal in squat, a silver medal in deadlift, and in bench press he took home the gold! He won four medals in all, the fourth a silver for accumulative achievement. (He lifted a cumulative total of 1,155 pounds in those events that day.)

Seth's bronze medal-winning squat at the
2018 Special Olympics USA Games in Seattle, WA

Nobody knew it, but Seth was injured the day he competed at the Special Olympics. He had pulled a hamstring and couldn't train for a couple of months before the competition. Still, the strength Seth had built up and maintained after his accident was staggering. He was breaking the chains of every limitation that had been spoken over him in the hospital. I had high expectations for him, knowing God could perform miracles, but all these accomplishments, especially in such a short time, exceeded my expectations. *All God.* Absolutely. All God.

Chapter 13

MARKS OF STRENGTH

"So we are convinced that every detail of our lives is continually woven together for good, for we are his lovers who have been called to fulfill his designed purpose"

— Romans 8:28 (TPT).

Seth's world was changing. He was tearing apart that list of "nots" and "nevers" and continuing to push through it despite ongoing difficulties and setbacks. Through it all, he joined me in giving glory to God as we both knew He was the one providing Seth with the strength, ability, and opportunities he was experiencing. God put people in our lives to help guide us along the way. Seth's genuine relationship with the Lord was not only intact, but I could see it growing deeper and stronger as he depended on his heavenly Father at every turn. He started each day by talking to his best friend. He knew just where (and from Whom) his strength came. Out of his gratefulness to the Lord, Seth had a strong desire to tell his story and bless others by pointing them to Him. One way he felt he could do this was by getting tattoos.

A year or so before his accident, Seth had bugged us about getting a tattoo. We weren't against the idea, but his dad and

I felt he was too young at the time and told him he needed to wait until he turned 18. His desire hadn't waned in that time, so after much planning, he got busy with the ink.

In addition to tattoos, Seth also has quite a few physical scars that he can point at to help tell his story. We have often referred to Seth's scars as "marks of strength." Some of them have now been tattooed over, but they are still visible and forever a part of him. Seth's scars and tattoos are his testimony on display for all to see, each tattoo bearing a significant meaning of what God has done in his life. Intrigued by his ink, many strangers approach Seth to ask about his tattoos. They serve as conversation starters, allowing him to share his story.

Seth got his first tattoo on his right shoulder on the first anniversary of his accident. It is an image of a man with wings rising up and breaking free from ropes that had him bound. On the man's chest is the word *Invictus*, Latin for unconquered. In the man's right hand is a cross, representing the call of God on Seth's life. He holds a dead serpent in his left hand, representing the enemy's defeat. Underneath each of the man's wings are the words *Percussus* (on the left) and *Resurgo* (on the right), the Latin phrase meaning, "When struck down, I will rise again." Underneath the image of the man is the scripture we prayed from the moment we received the news about Seth's accident: Psalms 118:17 (KJV): *"I shall not die, but live, and declare the works of the Lord."* Beneath the Scripture is the Latin phrase, *Carpe Diem*, meaning, Seize the Day. It is a philosophy to live your life today, so there are no regrets tomorrow.

On Seth's left shoulder is a cross in the center of tribal wings bearing Seth's version of Romans 8:28 underneath: *It's all good.*

Seth told his youth group he started out every morning reading that scripture. He even used it in his sermon the night before his accident, "Nothing the enemy does to you can stop the purpose and destiny God has placed inside of you," he told the congregation. How ironic that he got hit the next day. Over time we began to see that Seth's words were profoundly true. When the accident left him unresponsive in a coma, it surely looked like his purpose had been derailed, but that wasn't the end of his story.

On the inside of Seth's right forearm is a large cross bearing the Latin phrase *Primo Dios*, meaning, "God is first in my life." This statement rings true for people as they spend time with Seth. When he receives applause and accolades for his effort and accomplishments, he points upward to let people know it's all God. He's always careful to take no praise for himself. He gives the Lord the praise because he knows it's God's power at work in him, and He is all that really matters.

Remember, when he was struck from behind, he caved the van's hood, hit the windshield, and was thrown 167 feet before landing against a concrete guardrail. Though they didn't give up on doing all they could for Seth, none of the first responders expected him to survive. Seth coded twice on the scene with the paramedics before being life-flighted to Shreveport. So, there are two wings tattooed on the back of Seth's forearms, symbolizing that he died twice.

Seth's right arm has a tattoo of Jesus standing on the back of the grim reaper. Christ is lifting an unconscious Seth out of the grave with one hand and holding a spear in his other hand. The spear is aimed at the grim reaper's head, who is pictured crawling out of the grave and holding onto one of Seth's ankles.

Seth's tattoo testimony

The tombstone bears Seth's initials and the date of the accident. This is often the first tattoo Seth points to when someone asks him what happened. He pulls out his phone to show them a picture of himself in the hospital, then points to the tombstone and says, "Date."

On his lower left arm is the face of God watching over an image of Seth walking through the Valley of the Shadow of Death. In the image, Seth is holding a shield bearing a cross in one hand and a sword in the other. At his feet are skulls and bones with the words, "No Fear." On the other side of that forearm is an excerpt from Psalms 23: "Yea, though I walk through the Valley of the Shadow of Death, Thou art with me."

Seth's mantra is also a part of his tattoo testimony: *Quitting lasts forever, pain lasts for a moment, So Push Through It!* The first two lines are featured over his right shoulder, with the last line over his left shoulder.

Strength and Honor

Seth also has the word "Strength" tattooed on his left bicep and "Honor" on his right. He chose these words based on leadership principles he studied as a child from the book, *The Centurion's Principles,* written by Colonel Jeff O'Leary. The impact this book had on him was evident in his character and is perhaps best explained by the following excerpt:

"It describes a battle-hardened legionnaire who was promoted to the rank of Centurion based on at least sixteen

years of combat service and valor at the point of the spear. He was able to carry ninety pounds of equipment at least twenty miles per day and train under the harshest of conditions.

Centurions were required to equip themselves at their own expense and pay for their own food, clothing, bedding, boots, arms, armor, and pay dues to the burial club. A Centurion was a skilled engineer and builder, in addition to being the finest combat soldier. He held ultimate sway over the welfare of every person who served in his hundred-man century. To rise to Centurion was considered the highest privilege a legionnaire could attain.

The Centurion ate last, awoke first, and always led his troops from the front.

As you can see, there was no easy way to become a Centurion. It was not a role that could be purchased, appointed, or directed. It required complete and total dedication to a singular purpose. It demanded commitment, persistence, and above all, selflessness. Seasoned by harsh and often brutal experiences over a long period of time, earning the title centurion was a direct byproduct of consistently exercising the mental, emotional, and physical "strength" and unwavering dignity, integrity, and personal "honor" to lead a life of unwavering character."

O Death Where Is Your Sting?

People often ask Seth which tattoo is his favorite. When they do, it doesn't matter where we are or who is around; he will quickly take off his shirt to show his right pectoral muscle! It bears the image of Seth with his arm around the grim reaper's neck in a chokehold. He then proceeds to repeatedly flex his pectoral muscle, animating the tattoo version of himself choking out the grim reaper. From there, he'll point to his left pec featuring the scripture 1 Corinthians 15:55: *"O death, where is your sting, O grave where is victory?"*

Many people try to cover up their scars. For some, they serve as an ugly reminder of a painful event and are viewed as disfigured imperfections. Seth wears his scars as a badge of honor. They are proof he showed up on the battlefield and survived. He has never tried to hide them. In fact, he often wears tank tops to proudly display them.

It amazes me how God has used Seth's scars to minister to others. The scars and tattoos harmonize beautifully, giving God glory through Seth's tattoo story. They open a door for him to share his testimony time and again. Even without his full speech, Seth gets his message across. Besides his tattoos, he uses videos and pictures on his phone to tell his story. When we cross paths with someone with scars, tattoos, or an obvious disability, Seth approaches them without hesitation to ask what happened. He knows God placed them on his path for a reason, and he never fails to ask if he can pray for them and leave them with a hug.

People who engage with Seth generally assume that he was in the military. His tattoos are interesting and capture people's attention, but perhaps they gravitate toward him also because they believe he was in the service. He certainly looks like he has fought in numerous battles, and he has, just not the kind they're thinking of! One day, Seth approached a guy who, we found out, was a Marine. He engaged the man with a simple, "How are you?" (a phrase he learned how to say), and that's all it took. The man asked if Seth was in the military, and when he told him, "No," Seth began telling his story by bringing up his videos and pointing to his tattoos. The man looked on, spellbound. He started asking Seth questions. Then this young man began to open up to Seth and shared that he was a Marine and had recently gotten out of the service. He told him that he had lost some of his buddies in Afghanistan and was also injured himself.

There's beauty in your brokenness and a greater purpose to your pain.

As he shared a bit of his experience, he started bawling, telling Seth how hard it was losing his friends and about the survivor's guilt he was now left with. The two embraced, and the Marine said he knew their encounter was a gift from God. "Talking with you and seeing you helps me to know that I'll get through this. I just have to fight. I can't give in." What a raw and meaningful encounter that was!

I have seen grown men and women weep in public on many other occasions. Yes, because they are moved by Seth's story, but they are more deeply moved by him taking the time to ask about theirs. His boldness gives them the courage to share their own story. Just as Seth gave them hope, they realize they could be used to do the same for someone else.

There's beauty in your brokenness and a greater purpose to your pain. Every time you share your story, you not only bring healing to others, but healing pours back into you in return. What story do your scars tell? Someone needs to hear it today. Be bold. Be brave. Be healed.

If you are a caregiver, you bear your own scars; what comes with them is an important story to share. Your scars may not be physical, but as you have endured and labored, emotional scars have certainly formed. So, the charge to be bold, brave, and healed also applies to you. Someone needs to hear your story, too. Spread hope.

Chapter 14

SAYING WHAT NEEDED TO BE SAID

"Honesty is often very hard. The truth is often painful.
But the freedom it can bring is worth the trying."

— Fred Rogers

The hard and fast theme of Seth's recovery, almost since day one, as you know by now, has always been hope. That nurse fed me hope the day I received the list of "nots" and "nevers," and I have been spreading the news of hope as often as I could in many different venues. With Seth by my side, I began speaking to military and medical groups, universities, and churches, to name a few. I continue to book speaking engagements to inspire, challenge, and encourage others to carry that torch of hope—this has included talking to the doctors of patients suffering from traumatic brain injury (TBI). In my experience, some medical professionals seemed to only consider medical science and nothing beyond, leaving little (if any) room for hope. This was both unfair and untrue in our experience.

One of the most amazing feelings for me—as if I had crossed the finish line after running a long marathon—was when I returned to the Children's Hospital over a year after Seth's accident. I found the doctor who had held up that model of a brain in that dark conference room and asked if I could have a few minutes of his time. "I want to show you how Seth is doing now," I said. Seth stood beside me, all dressed up in a black suit, looking sharp. He was smiling his beautiful, crooked grin because his face was still paralyzed at that point. The doctor looked at him and responded with, "Wow! Look at you! We did a good job!" And I stopped him right there. "You said he would never ever be able to walk unassisted, talk, open his right hand, understand humor, know his family, remember anything from his past...." I went on and on down the list of "nots" and "nevers" he had recited for me when Seth was his patient.

Some positive visits that happened that first year or so after Seth's accident included meeting Rusty. He was the helicopter pilot who airlifted Seth to the trauma center that fateful day. (It was approximately a 25-minute flight). We flew in that same helicopter to let Seth see what it was like to be up in the sky like that, this time fully conscious! During the afternoon with Rusty, we told him about what God had done in Seth's life in just one year and thanked him for the part he played in saving his life. (We began celebrating the anniversary of Seth's accident each year, and we continue this tradition to celebrate his life. Since he died twice and came back to life, we call September 28th his "re-birthday.")

We also got in touch with Jessica, one of the EMTs who was instrumental in reviving Seth twice at the scene of the accident. She now works as an instructor and shows a video about Seth as she trains new EMTs. She uses Seth's story to remind them to never give up—no matter how hopeless the situation may look. His miraculous story so significantly impacted Jessica that she got her own tattoo depicting what happened at the scene. We wanted to make sure she knew what a difference she made and how grateful we will forever be for her. We've seen her several times since Seth's accident, and when we've tried to thank her for all she did for him, she tells us, "It's all God."

And, about two or three years after the accident, we crossed paths with the state trooper who was first on the scene. Seth's dad had pulled into a gas station one afternoon and was filling up his tank with Seth in the car when he saw the officer and recognized him. He approached the man and asked if he was the one who helped our son that day on the highway. The officer had no trouble remembering September 28, 2011, the call he had responded to, and what he encountered when he came onto the scene. It was still etched clearly in his mind. Seth got out of the car to greet the man, and when the state trooper laid eyes on him, he became emotional. He knew that the fact that Seth was living, breathing, and very much alive was a true miracle.

During all these "reunions," we wanted to let each person know the difference they made in our lives and the countless others we were able to encourage. I was on a mission to let the first responders, medical staff, and everyone that showed up for Seth and put effort into his survival and recovery know that what they did mattered, and we thanked God for them. I was sure that many wondered what had become of that young man whose situation seemed so hopeless. When we had these encounters, each one (except for a few doctors) expressed their thankfulness to not only learn of his survival but of the miraculous healing he was experiencing. Many would say, "I've often wondered what became of Seth, and I'm so thankful to know now." They also appreciated being appreciated! Whenever we were in Shreveport and New Orleans for appointments, we would stop by LSU Trauma Center and the Children's Hospital and remind the staff they were making a difference. Encouragement is crucial for everyone—our whole family needed it while Seth was in the hospital, and they needed it regarding their everyday work.

I also wanted to remind them of something else: to keep exercising compassion. Sometimes medical staff can get tunnel vision regarding their different tasks and duties. Of course, they need to guard their emotions, but compassion cannot be lost in the shuffle. I told them that their investment in Seth's life was being multiplied countless times as Seth's testimony touched many people's lives. He was bringing hope, inspiration, and encouragement to others. While still in the hospital and at every doctor's appointment (and it seemed like there were thousands) following his discharge, I would tell the medical staff, "You're touching one person's life today who will touch thousands of people." I somehow knew early on that Seth would have an impact and watching how that has played out continues to thrill me. The kindness bestowed upon Seth and our family by those we encountered in the hospital was a life preserver. Those who didn't exercise compassion made our difficult situation that much harder. Compassion matters.

Seven years after Seth was airlifted to the trauma center, I finally met up with the other doctor who had told me we needed to put Seth in an institution. Like the encounter with the surgeon I had mentioned earlier, this didn't go as I had hoped, but I believe it was positive in a more significant and, hopefully, far-reaching way.

By the time I saw her again, Seth had been living a full life and was accomplishing a great deal. He was competing as a powerlifter and representing the state of Louisiana in the Special Olympics. He had gone back to college and received his certification in relaxation therapy. He was running in marathons and driving a car again. With Seth by my side this time, we boldly approached the doctor, and I asked her if she remembered him. She stared at him momentarily, trying to recollect who he was and the circumstances surrounding his hospital stay.

I couldn't blame her for struggling. Seth didn't look anything like he did seven years earlier. By this time, he had filled out, and both his arms were fully tattooed. He was now six feet tall, having grown four inches since he was her patient. She continued to study him and then finally exclaimed, "Oh, my gosh, yes! I remember him now. Wow!" Then, like the other neurosurgeon I had confronted years earlier, she acted as if she should take credit for his miraculous recovery and accomplishments. Ironically, we were standing in front of the same room that Seth was in for much of his early days in ICU. I pointed to it and said, "Seth was here seven years ago in that very room. You told us when he came out of his coma that we should institutionalize him. Then, a week later, you told us that whatever he is in a year is all he'll ever be. You said his brain would not progress past that point if he progresses at all." I was on a roll, so I continued. "I just want you to know that people in our situation need more than what you know medically. We need something to hold onto to give us some hope." Her eyes widened as I spoke to her. I was fired up, for sure. The nurses within earshot heard my rant, and the looks on their faces told me they were glad she got served. It was obvious that her *modus operandi,* which we had experienced while Seth was her patient, had continued with other patients, and those who worked with her knew it wasn't right.

I don't want to sound mean-spirited, but I made no apologies for what I said to that doctor that day or the doctor I had confronted years earlier. I passionately believed that they needed to learn to give patients like Seth and their families a measure of hope. After all, that is reality. Medical science is impressive and essential, but there is more to treatment than what science can offer. There are possibilities beyond what is found in a medical textbook. Seth was living proof, and I wanted them to recognize it for the sake of their future patients and their families. In this way, I advocated for those who would come after us.

It's All A Part of the Job

One thing that became abundantly clear after Seth's accident (and continues to this day) is that I needed to be on my toes and advocate for him in many different situations. For example, many mainstream doctors don't hesitate to push and prescribe medication. A lot of medication! I found that if a doctor felt there was a pill that could fix a medical problem Seth was experiencing, then, "I'll write him a prescription," became their typical response and solution. He was given loads of meds in many forms in the hospital and prescribed all kinds of meds when we brought him home and from then on. Some were necessary, but not all, and even then, some were only necessary for a time. I had to be aware of the possible side effects of the different medications so I could appropriately question doctors (I'm sure sometimes doctors felt like I was inappropriately questioning them!) and advocate for my son.

Over the years, this has led me to conduct my own research and make some decisions for Seth regarding different medications. For example, a common scenario looked something like this: A medicine he needed to take caused stomach issues, so he would be prescribed another med to soothe his gut. That new med calmed his stomach, but a side effect was insomnia, so he would be given meds to help him sleep. A side effect of that medication would cause diarrhea...You get the picture. Before we knew it, Seth would be taking a handful of meds when,

> *Medical science is impressive and essential, but there is more to treatment than what science can offer. There are possibilities beyond what is found in a medical textbook.*

at times, the best thing to do was take him off the initial medication and allow his body to adjust and heal itself. However, taking him off meds has never been done flippantly. In addition to doing research, I have always sought medical advice, and I've learned to get a second opinion. I've also used many homeopathic remedies as well. All this is just a part of the job of being a caregiver and advocate.

I have also learned to inform every nurse, doctor, and medical staff helping Seth about what happened to him. I have made it a point to tell his story to nurses just starting their shift and then retell it when the next nurse begins her shift and enters Seth's room. Why? To fight against any stereotyping that may be going on. Because of his appearance, people can easily assume that Seth must have been doing something wrong or shady to be in the shape he's in. They can think a bad thing happened to him as a consequence, something he deserved somehow. Of course, nothing could be further from the truth. But, it's our human nature to size up someone and make unfair judgments about them based on their appearance. Assumptions like this are out of ignorance, but none of us are immune to making them, even professional nurses and doctors. So, I always greet the person assigned to help Seth with, "Hi, thank you for taking care of my son. Let me tell you his story...." Otherwise, how would they know how hard he's fought to get to where he is now? Seth was unable to tell his story. If I don't do it, who will?

Being an advocate isn't for the faint of heart. It takes some chutzpah and determination. If being bold and confident isn't your natural personality, my advice is to pray and ask God to equip you to do what needs to be done and give you favor with those you must deal with on behalf of your loved one. As wonderful as most doctors and nurses are, they can be intimidating. They are also human and, therefore, fallible. So, don't be afraid to speak up just because you don't have a medical degree. As your loved one's caregiver, you will often instinctively know when something is wrong, even if a doctor brushes you off. Continue to advocate for them. Sure, you could be wrong in your assessment, but what if you're right? So, summon your courage and speak up. "Fake it 'til you make it" may need to be your mantra at first to build your boldness. Use some acting skills if you need to, and practice not being unnerved when you must approach them or speak with anyone you need to help you. Be kind but firm. Respectful but steadfast. You having the courage to speak up could make a positive and even life-saving difference for the one who is ultimately in your care.

Some other practical advice as you advocate for your loved one is to educate yourself regarding their rights when it comes to compensation, accommodation, and more. For example, when Seth went back to school after his accident, I had to learn what was legally in place in "the system" and make sure that everything he had the right to was made available to him. More often than not, the many resources available are not fully disclosed. You have to dig for it, and once you know your loved one's rights, you most likely will have to fight for them. (I must warn you that you may not win any popularity contests at this point, but that's okay. That's not what being an advocate is about.) Making sure Seth was given the accommodations he needed to earn the certification he was working toward took a lot of back-and-forth with the powers that be, but he finally received his due! It was more than worth it watching him walk across the stage to accept his degree in Massage Therapy!

It can be time-consuming and frustrating but, when necessary, do all you can to advocate for the survivor in your life. You may not win every battle, but your efforts will pay off over time. For instance, Seth was put on a waiting list called a "waiver," and it took eight years for him to finally get off the list

Seth graduating from college with
a degree in Massage Therapy (June 30, 2017)

and receive what was rightfully his! The waiver would give him more financial assistance for various needs and was important for his future, but there was so much red tape surrounding it that I had to exercise endurance in my fight to get it for him. Persistence paid off, though. It usually does. So, knock and keep knocking. Call and keep calling. Don't take the first "no." Push through it! Ask for the person in charge, take down names, and get extensions and direct numbers. (Another tip: Ask for it in writing! Request email confirmation of what was discussed.)

Be organized and develop a system that works for you. Maintain a paper trail to use as proof of promises, etc. Do all you can to prevent your loved one (and their needs) from falling through the cracks of an overburdened system. Your hard work will pay off, though it could take some time. Persevere. And, if you encounter changes that need to be made in "the system" of whatever you're dealing with—take it on if you can and be the voice for advocacy! When you do, you will not only help your loved one, but you could help many others who have no voice in the process.

Chapter 15

THE ARENA OF LIFE

"...let your light shine before others, so that
they may see your good works and give glory to
your Father who is in heaven"

— Matt. 5:16 ESV

As Seth continued to compete and participate in the Special Olympics, he had a real sense of purpose. He worked hard to accomplish his goals, and one of his greatest joys beyond the medals were the kids he was able to reach. He became a hero to many of them. They looked up to Seth and wanted to feel his muscles, get a hug, and cheer him on. With limited words but unlimited enthusiasm, Seth would encourage these kids and their families.

Now, seven years after his accident, he caught the attention of ESPN. This popular sports channel produced a ten-minute segment on Seth, telling his story from the time of his accident to his present-day involvement with the Special Olympics and interviewing him after he competed in the 2018 Special Olympic USA Games at the University of Washington. The segment showed Seth coming onto the field at the start of the Special Olympic ceremonies, carrying the flag for the state of Louisiana. It told the story of what happened to him on September 28, 2011, and his recovery journey. The video featured his three competitive lifts as well. They also published an article I wrote about him with one of their staff writers and featured it in ESPN's The Body Issue Magazine. ESPN stopped publishing the magazine in 2019, but it featured famous, accomplished athletes in the buff with their "parts" strategically covered (sort of). Seth was featured in a special edition for their tenth anniversary. They put a photo of him in the centerfold–fully clothed; thank you very much! There he was praying with Romans 8:28 (his favorite Scripture) proudly displayed on his tree-trunk biceps! We were thrilled for Seth and in awe of all God was doing in his life.

By this time, the Team Seth Foundation for Traumatic Brain

Seth's centerfold featured in the 10th Anniversary
edition of ESPN'S *The Body* Magazine

Injury Awareness was already posting videos featuring Seth on YouTube and Facebook. It didn't take long before he gained a following. People worldwide started reaching out letting us know how Seth (and his story) made a difference in their lives. Many we heard from had also been affected by a traumatic brain injury, either personally or through someone they loved and cared for. We heard from others, too. Most who commented on Seth's videos were in a fight of their own. They were battling issues that came with an injury or diagnosis. Some struggled with mental health challenges, while others were caregivers in great need of encouragement and support.

We recently started a TikTok channel. If you've ever watched one of our TikTok videos, you know that while we inform and educate viewers about traumatic brain injury, we also incorporate plenty of humor. We learned early on to find the "funny" in things. And guess what? Seth gets it! He not only understands humor but also dishes it out, proving again that medical science is limited. Rarely a day goes by when we don't laugh about something together. (Even when we're in the thick of a setback). Humor is therapeutic for us, so we share it with our viewers. There's a Jewish proverb that says, "As soap is to the body, so laughter is to the soul." Amen to that!

Knowing we are reaching people from around the globe has been invigorating. We love reading our messages and coming up with new videos to share. It takes some work, but it has been an activity worthy of our time and attention because it blesses people.

Participating on these platforms has never been about bringing glory to Seth or me. It began (and continues to be) a way to help others and turn tragedy into triumph for the glory of God. The fact that so many were responding to our posts and videos confirmed there was a need out there, and being a presence on social media was just one way to help meet it. We knew this was the case because, from the beginning of Seth's hospitalization, we had searched for stories online, trying to learn from those suffering from a traumatic brain injury who had a positive outcome, and we found very little.

We received regular communication from some who followed Seth or were new to his story, almost from the beginning. I could fill a whole book (or two!) with all the messages we've received over the years, but I'll give just a few examples. One person who reached out to us was a woman in Australia. She messaged us on TikTok and told us about her son, who had been born with aphasia. She said she used some of the ideas we posted and found them very helpful. For instance, in one of our posts, we showed the easiest way for Seth to order from a fast-food menu. We filmed him as he took a picture of the menu with his phone, enlarged it so the person behind the counter could see it, and then pointed to items he wanted. The woman went on to say that our practical and inspirational posts gave her hope that her son would be able to grow up to live a fairly normal life, even with his communication issues.

Another time, a military wife messaged us to say that her husband was serving in Kuwait. She told us that she had sent him one of our videos because he had friends suffering from traumatic brain injury and that he had sustained multiple concussions himself. As a result, he was struggling with depression and other side effects from his injuries. She said our video touched him and his unit so much that he wanted to give Seth a special gift. True to his word, he sent Seth an American flag that had been flown over Camp Arifjan's military base in Kuwait, a military challenge coin, and a dog tag with a note letting Seth know that he was inspiring hope all the way over in Kuwait. He (and his brothers and sisters in arms) appreciated Seth's story and were blessed by it.

Then there was a journalist from Mexico who was looking for support. She told us that her boyfriend Julio had been at a bar when he was struck with a beer bottle on the back of the head. He had checked on a girl at the bar after witnessing her boyfriend physically knocking her down. Julio went over to help her up and make sure she was alright. Out of jealousy and anger, her boyfriend came after Julio from behind and assaulted him. Instead of heading straight to the hospital, Julio made his way home and slipped into a coma. His brain was bleeding. Thankfully, he was given medical attention, and, like Seth, a large section of Julio's skull had to be removed. We ended up talking with this young man over Skype, and he told Seth, in his labored speech, "I'm going to become like you, Seth. I'm going to be a motivational speaker. I want to inspire people." Julio went on to do just that, and he even wrote a book about his experiences.

Our TikTok and YouTube presence have also opened doors for us to tell Seth's story in person in a variety of venues, including some universities where we've been able to speak to auditoriums filled with students. One of the topics we include in our talk is suicide. Though almost no one in the audience (made up mostly of young adult students) is struggling with a brain injury like Seth, many struggle in their own way and for different reasons. We want to give these students hope that they can overcome whatever challenges they're dealing with and that they don't have to give in to suicide. We also share that our hope goes beyond positive thinking and perseverance, though those things are essential. Our hope ultimately lies in Christ Jesus.

Three years after speaking at one of these university engagements, a young woman approached us wearing one of Seth's bracelets. (At each venue, we give out black and red bracelets with his mantra printed on them: "Quitting lasts forever, pain lasts for a moment... so PUSH THROUGH IT!") The bracelet on her wrist, however, had no words on it. She told us she had worn it for the past three years because his story and our message hugely impacted her life. The words may have rubbed off her bracelet, but they were imprinted on her heart.

> *The very thing you thought would kill you—yes, that painful place—is where ministry flows from.*

Remember, Seth's verbal input was very limited in all these encounters and during each speaking engagement. He still cannot articulate in words everything he would like. His speech lacks dimension, so when he communicates, he leaves out all of the fluff and filler words (adjectives, adverbs, and pronouns). It takes some charades, texts, and images he brings up on his phone for him to communicate intricate thoughts and feelings, but he puts in the effort because he wants to express himself. Most of the time, he gets his point across very well.

I absolutely believe Seth will, once again, speak clearly for all to hear, but while he waits, he continues to share the Gospel with limited vocabulary and through uncommon methods. However, he has impacted more people with no words than I believe he ever would have otherwise. And you can't help but be around Seth even for a minute and not quickly see how much he loves Jesus. It shows on his countenance, and you feel it in his spirit. His walk with Christ has inspired and encouraged complete strangers, leaving them hungry to know more about the God he serves. His faith is not just something he says; it is something he lives.

It would be easy for Seth to find a reason to be angry at the life that was taken from him. Every second of every day, he could live full of bitterness. He could be consumed by rage and blame God. He could use the excuse, "I can't communicate clearly. I'm the one who needs to be encouraged." Instead, he gives others what he desperately needs: prayers and encouragement. He always leaves them with a smile and a hug.

Seth unashamedly prays for people in public, boldly using the language he says God gave him when he died. You may not understand his words, but the power you feel when he prays is undeniable. So let me challenge you with this: Ask yourself, "What's my excuse?" If you have a relationship with Jesus, what's holding you back from sharing what Christ has done in your life? The very thing you thought would kill you—yes, that painful place—is where ministry flows from. (If you don't have a relationship with Christ and would like to, you will be guided through how to do that in Chapter 17.)

I want to say that whether or not you are in the public eye, your life is also on display for all to see. Many spectators sit in the grandstands watching as you battle through difficulties and victories. Some will cheer you on, while others hope you fall. With each passing year and each new battle, some will exit your arena. Don't try to convince them to stay. Let them go! They are simply making room for new people to take the seats they vacated.

It has been like this with Seth's story, or shall I say God's story. We play supporting roles as characters in it, but our Creator holds the pen in His hand. He continues to write His story for His glory through Seth's life. What a privilege to have a front-row seat and observe, at least in part, what God is doing.

Even with the positive things happening in Seth's life, he has still had to make a conscious effort to push through it. To push through the pain. To push through the disappointments. To push through the depression that hovers and threatens to envelop him. So I ask again: What's your excuse? You, like Seth, will be faced with many opportunities to quit. During those times, you will find out who you are at your core. Crisis reveals character, and you never know who is watching your story unfold. You never know how your story can be used in amazing ways in someone else's life.

What Doesn't Kill You Makes You Stronger

Seth was still training and competing as a powerlifter when a representative from the Paralympics contacted him. The first conversation we had over the phone was somewhat comical.

The representative told me they were interested in having Seth compete—not in powerlifting, but track and field! She said he would be required to qualify in the regional, national, and international competitions to be eligible to travel with the U.S.A. Team, and they felt that he had a real chance. My jaw dropped, not because I didn't think she was right—I knew Seth could do it—but because this opportunity was so unexpected. She asked me, "Has he ever thrown a shot put?" I told her I had no idea what that was! My answer didn't deter her in the least. Her enthusiasm over Seth never waned when she asked if he'd ever thrown a discus, and I had to honestly say, "No, and

Crisis reveals character.

I don't know what that is either!" "Ok, well, no worries," she replied, "you can look it up later. Pull up some videos on the Paralympics, and you'll see. He'll need to start training. I'll go ahead and send you the dates and some information. I cannot wait for the U.S.A. Olympic Team to meet Seth!"

When I hung up the phone, I thought, "This is it! This is the 'why' right here." Being a part of the Paralympics would mean that he would train and travel with the Olympic and Paralympic Teams. Competing for the Special Olympics was a huge honor, but it isn't the Olympics; it's a separate entity. The Paralympics, however, are part of the Olympics and on the world stage. Being on the Paralympic Team would mean that Seth would go to the Olympic Training Center in Colorado Springs to train with a coach and other teammates. He would have sponsors and actually make some money. (We had to raise funds for him and others to compete in the Special Olympics.) He was excited about the possibility of earning a paycheck and being independent. He looked forward to competing and continuing to be challenged. We also knew that his platform to tell others his story and share his faith would grow dramatically. We would be able to share his story with a broader audience and show the world that a traumatic brain injury is not necessarily a death sentence.

Seth quickly threw himself into training. He had a goal like never before and was ready to get after it. Having no doubt he would succeed, I did everything I could to support him. He soon competed in the regionals and made the B Team at that time, even though he was new to track and field! (There are A, B, and C teams in these competitions). In April, the following month, he was headed to the nationals. Two weeks later, he was expected to advance to the international round to qualify for the Paralympic Team. In addition to preparing for the Paralympics, he was preparing for the Special Olympics division of a World Powerlifting Competition. Seth was busy like never before, but he was enjoying himself, and the possibilities ahead of him were endless. All this kept me busy, too, as I managed his schedule and ensured he got to wherever he needed to be.

And then, without warning, everything took a turn in a much different direction.

It was March 1, 2019, Seth's birthday. We had just gone out to dinner to celebrate, and when we got back home, he began insisting, yet again, that he shave his head. He'd been bugging me about it relentlessly for several weeks. I've always loved Seth's beautiful, curly hair, but off and on for years after his accident, he kept wanting to shave it off. I had been able to talk him out of it until now. To be honest, besides loving his curls, I also didn't want people to see the many scars on his head and treat him like he was a freak. I'd experienced how cruel people could be, stereotyping those with disabilities and severe scars. I knew I couldn't shield him from that, but why make the scar stand out more than it needed to? So, each time he'd bring up shaving his head, I'd fight him on the idea and win. I'd also try and reason with him. "Girls love curls," I'd say, appealing to his Casanova side, which had not disappeared after his brain injury. (As is evident from his TikTok, that side of him was very much alive and well). He was determined, however, and once Seth makes up his mind to do something, it's only a matter of time before it happens.

He tried to get me to help him shave his head, but I refused. (I can be stubborn, too!) That didn't stop him, however. Seth went into his bathroom and turned on the electric razor. It wasn't long before I heard him loudly exclaim, "Oh crap!" I ran to his bathroom, thinking something was wrong, and when I got there, I couldn't help but laugh. Seth had made a valiant attempt to shave his head but ended up looking like he had mange. I gave him a good-natured tongue lashing, as only a momma can, and then helped shave all the patches of hair, going very slowly and carefully near his scar. As I did, we noticed an opening on the left side of his head where the craniotomy had been done. His determination to shave his head turned out to be a God thing. It was only because he insisted on cutting his hair that day that we discovered he was leaking brain fluid.

We found the leak over the weekend, so we had to wait until Monday morning to get Seth to the neurologist. At our appointment, the neurologist quickly confirmed our fears, and we were told that a deep tissue skin graft would have to be done to close the wound. We were also told that Seth needed to stop everything. His training had to end. He was not to pick up anything heavier than a milk jug, and he needed to have surgery as soon as possible. The surgeon determined Seth's right forearm was the most viable area to harvest the graft. Ironically, it already had a tattoo of the grim reaper. The skin bearing the tattoo of the grim reaper's head was transferred just behind his left temple to cover the wound.

Sounds so simple, right? Not so.

When someone has a skin graft harvested, they have to endure the same pain and treatment as someone with a third-degree burn would (including hydrotherapy). Seth had to spend several nights in the Burn ICU. He was on such a strong regimen of IV antibiotics, it adversely affected his veins. The IV kept "blowing," and nurses had to move it several times each day. The nurses had so much trouble with his veins blowing, they eventually called an anesthesiologist to stick his foot. After blowing through both feet and several days of this repetitive and excruciating process, the doctor finally allowed them to remove the IV. Since Seth was scheduled to be released the following day, they started him on oral antibiotics.

After he was discharged, they sent a "wound vac" home for the deep tissue skin graft on his forearm. He had weekly debridement appointments where doctors removed the damaged and dead tissue from the wounds on his thigh and forearm. (They

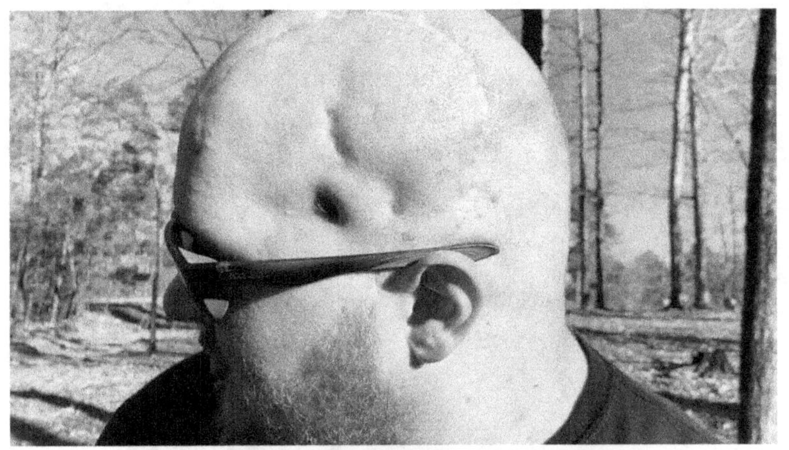

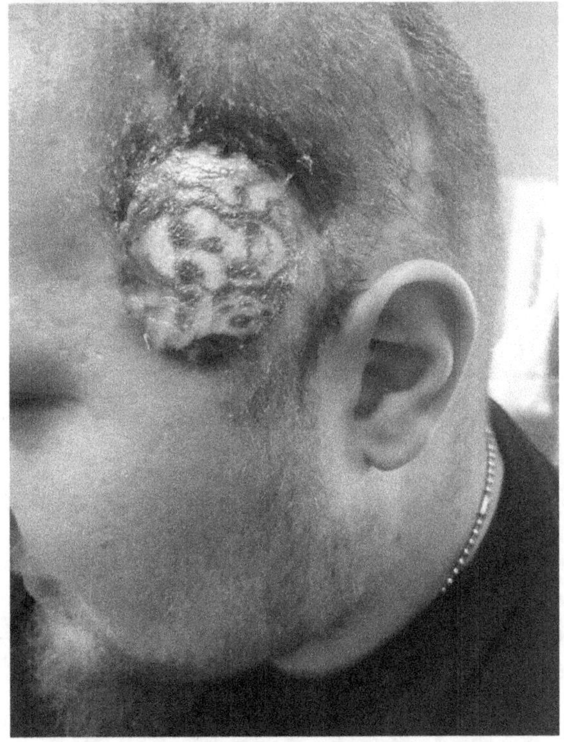

Seth before the skin graft and after the grim reaper
tattoo had been transferred

also took a large skin graft from his right thigh to replace where they took the deep tissue graft from his forearm). The part that was hardest for me to watch was when they would insert the needle into his forearm to draw off vials of fluid. Seth has a high tolerance for pain after all he's been through. He always tries to be tough and put on a good front. But even he couldn't hide the pain during these treatments. He would tremble uncontrollably as they drew the fluid off.

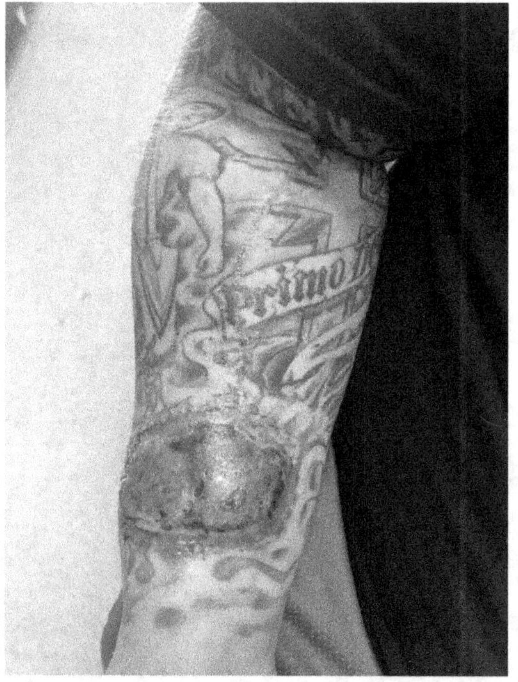

Seth's right forearm where his deep tissue skin graft was harvested

Throughout it all, Seth never lost his sense of humor. The wound on his arm looked disgusting during the healing process. When people would ask what happened, Seth would say,

"Zombie," followed by his version of charades, growling and acting like he was biting his arm as he demonstrated.

Though we were thankful to have discovered the leak when we did, we were devastated as all our plans and Seth's hard work training and competing to qualify for the Paralympics—all his dreams and my dreams for him—were once again slipping away. He was on the brink of this incredible opportunity, and now this! I was so sure that his becoming an Olympian answered the "why" to all he had gone through up to this point. In a small but significant way, it seemed it could redeem some of the heartache and pain of what he had lived through. So, now what? Here was yet another situation where our faith in God and hope in His plans would be put to the test. Could we trust God with this new disappointment and new setback?

I must say that through this experience, I've forever changed my outlook on scars. Now I say, don't hide your scars because the story of how they came to be is too painful to talk about. They are badges of honor—evidence that you survived something that almost killed you. Seth Hanchey is covered from head to toe with battle scars. They prove that he fought a battle (several battles, actually) with Death and won! Like a gladiator holding up the head of his conquered foe, Seth now had the head of death displayed for all to see. Anyone who dared stereotype or treat him like a freak would only show their ignorance. Seth was alive, which made him victorious, and that's all that mattered.

His recovery after this surgery was slow. He had to stay several days in the hospital and then, when he was released, had plenty more healing to do from home. Once again, I made it my mission to encourage Seth during this time. His physical pain was ever-present, and disappointment over having to give up his chance with the Olympics was palpable. I would cheer him on, talk him through the countless difficult moments, and then hide in the bathroom and bawl my eyes out. How many more setbacks and disappointments could we take? The answer I didn't want to think about was: more. Sure enough, another significant one was on its way.

Chapter 16

PERCEPTION CHANGES EVERYTHING

"When we shift our perception, our experience changes."

— Lindsay Wagner

What do you see when you look at these four letters— F.E.A.R.? Did you see the word FEAR? Did it immediately make you feel vulnerable and think of something terrible that could happen? Or something that already has? The word FEAR is not what it seems at first glance. It's actually an acronym for Face Everything and Rise (or, Face Everything and Run). It's all in how you perceive it.

I lived many years following Seth's accident, oppressed and smothered by fear. Like a boxer in a ring, I was constantly braced for the next painful blow. It was exhausting. I knew my fear was keeping me locked up tight in a straitjacket, but I did not have the Houdini-like skills to get myself loose. Fear and insecurity had me in a stranglehold.

There have been times Seth did something that would ignite my fear, fanning the dread in me of something happening that would make his life (and mine) even more challenging. Ultimately, I was afraid he might do something to get himself killed. It is not uncommon for traumatic brain injury survivors to have a skewed outlook on life. In Seth's case, the main factor of his impaired judgment was that he felt invincible. Since God had spared him from his accident, and Seth had cheated death twice when he coded, what could touch him now? Umm...plenty.

On the fifth anniversary of Seth's accident, we took him to our remote cabin in the mountains of Arkansas. It was his first time back there since the accident. One morning, at the crack of dawn, and while we were still sleeping, Seth got out of bed and left the cabin. He hopped onto our four-wheeler and took off by himself down the gravel road. There were no street signs or neighbors for many miles in either direction from where our cabin was located. It was surrounded by acres and acres of rustic wilderness. When we woke up and couldn't find Seth in the house, we went outside and discovered that not only was he gone, but so was the four-wheeler. We freaked out, as you can imagine. We had no idea how long he had been gone.

I immediately called his cell phone, and by some miracle, he had cell coverage. When he answered my call, he could only say, "Help, help. Help me." It was evident by the tone of his voice that he was in deep distress. With my heart beating out of my chest, I asked him what had happened. He couldn't tell me. I asked him to tell me where he was, but he didn't know. He wasn't able to tell me which direction he had traveled. Since there were no street signs and he couldn't provide me with landmarks, we were clueless about where he could be. Even if these things were in place and he knew where he was, he couldn't form enough words at the time to communicate. Understanding his limited speech in person was one thing, but over the phone made it ten times more difficult.

I was panicking at this point but told him as calmly as I could to stay on the phone with me. Then his dad and I jumped into our truck to look for him, but we had no idea where to start! I asked Seth, "When you came out of the driveway, which way did you turn, left or right?" Again, he couldn't tell me, so we just drove, praying we were headed in the best direction and would find our son. We scoured the area, going around the top of the mountain on the lookout for Seth, all the while asking him questions but getting nowhere. It was hard to think rationally; I was so afraid. Finally, I asked, "Were you headed home, or had you turned to go the other way?" His reply came: "Home, home." As we drove around the bluff at the top of the mountain, we came to a section of the road with a sharp curve that immediately went into a steep decline. As we rounded the turn, there was our four-wheeler! It was turned on its side in the middle of the road, and the tires were still spinning.

Dust from the gravel road billowed in the air like an S.O.S. smoke signal. We could tell Seth had taken the curve too fast, was thrown from the vehicle, and tumbled over the edge. I was terrified at what I would find as I peered down that bluff. There was Seth, caught in briars that grew particularly full this time of year. With their two-inch thorns, these briars "caught" Seth's body like a spider web catching a fly and kept him from falling down the mountain.

Had this happened a few months earlier, the briars would not have been so prolific. Seth's life had been saved by a plant forming a web of thorns, which (ironically) are called Christ

Plant or Crown of Thorns. How appropriate! (Don't ever doubt that God has a sense of humor!) Thankfully Seth was awake. He told us he had tried to climb up the bluff, but he blacked out and fell back down. He was bleeding from a large gash on his head and cheek. It was not safe for us to help him out of the web, so we had to be careful. We quickly strategized, and between the two of us, we pulled him out and back onto the road. We knew we couldn't just take him back to the cabin to tend to his wounds. We were more concerned about injuries he might have sustained that we could not see, primarily because of his already-present brain injury. He had hit his head on his fall, so we had to keep him awake in case he had a concussion. Once you acquire a brain injury, you are more susceptible or at a higher risk of sustaining or acquiring another one. It also halts the synapsis or whatever new growth or healing is already in the process for the initial injury. We needed to get him to the hospital.

We knew because Seth had a brain injury that we couldn't go to just any hospital. We had to get to one equipped with a skilled neurologist or neurosurgeon, even if it meant not driving to the nearest hospital. We went to the closest hospital to our house back in Louisiana, a four-and-a-half-hour drive away. After being examined there, we were put at ease that, although he was bruised, battered, and cut, his shunt had not been affected. I'm sure I lost a few years off of my life that fearful day, but Seth was okay.

Another incident that ignited fresh fear in me happened about two years later near our home. We were preparing to host our third 5K run for The Team Seth Foundation, and Seth had

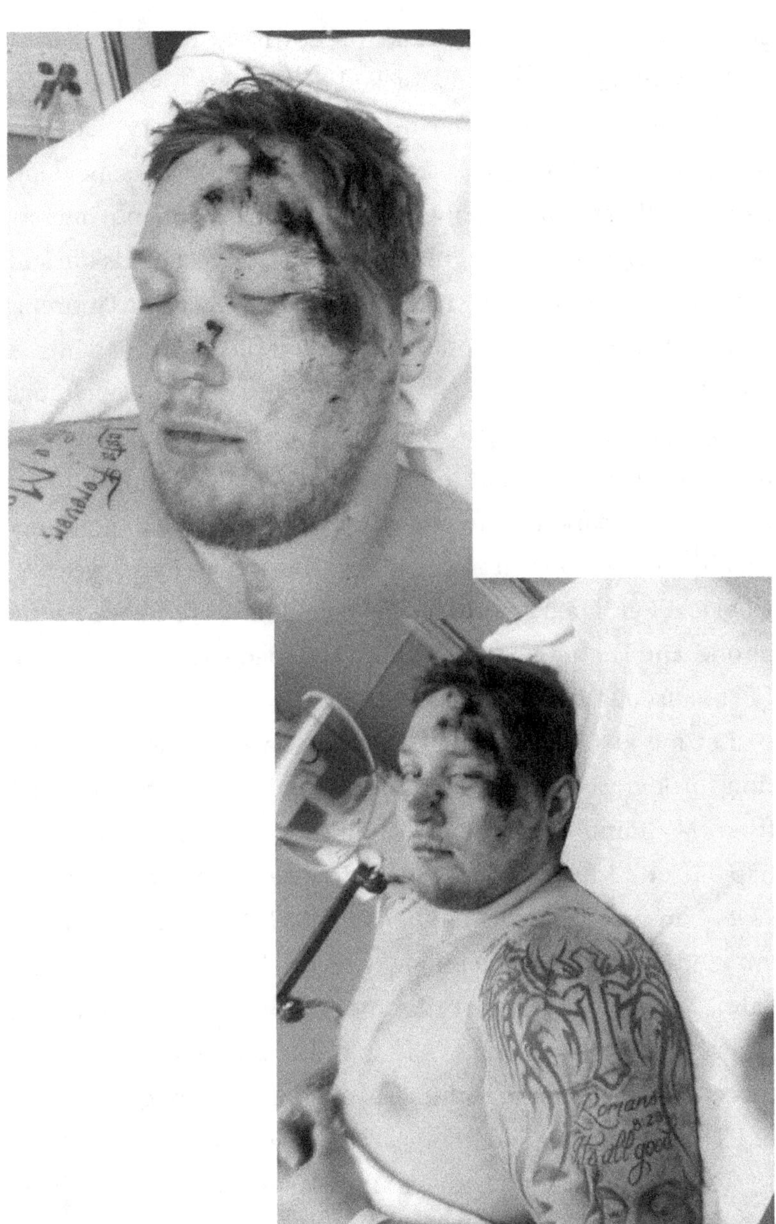

Seth in the ER after his four-wheeler accident

gone on a training run. As he set off down our cul-de-sac, a pit bull tore off after him and attacked him, biting his inner thigh and barely missing his groin area and the main artery. Seth was not doing anything reckless at the time, but after this incident, I kept thinking that the only way to protect my son moving forward was to wrap him in bubble wrap for the rest of his life and lock him in a closet! Can you blame me? But there was more…

Another time after that, Seth went for a run in a park just a few miles from our house. It was still daylight when he left, but it got dark quickly. To get to the park, he had to run along the main highway for part of the way, and when we realized that it had become dark and he was still out, we panicked. Not only was he not wearing his lighted vest, but he was also wearing all black. I grabbed my phone and called him. He answered the phone, and I could hear the cars on the road swishing past him. I felt nauseous, beside myself with fear.

Let me just say here that when you are filtering information through the lens of PTSD, you are dealing with a warped filter. My mind was racing with all the "what-ifs" that could happen, and I felt like I was going to lose it. I had experienced severe anxiety since September 28, 2011, but this was different. Seth was still on the phone with me, but I couldn't remain calm. Whatever hit me at that moment was like something I had never known before, as the sound of the cars triggered my fears. The noise of the traffic was magnified through the filter of PTSD, so in my mind, there were cars all around him.

The reality was that Seth was fine. He wasn't hurt. He wasn't in trouble or any kind of distress. But, as his dad and I once again had to hop into the truck to look for him, I had a major freak-out episode. I kept thinking about how easy it would be for someone driving their car near Seth to hit him and finish him off. All it would take was for a driver to look down at their phone for a split second and swerve just barely, and that would be the end of him. My body shook as I leaned forward to look out the window, squinting my eyes to try and find my son. Finally, we spotted him, but we could *barely* see him and were intentionally looking for him! This only confirmed my fear that he was a sitting duck for anyone who wasn't fully paying attention to the road. I felt my fear

> *If you live your life always braced for the next bad thing to happen, it's like holding your breath and never exhaling. Eventually, you will stop breathing and stop living.*

and anger escalating until they enveloped me. *It's dark! He's not wearing a vest!* I knew what could happen. *The unthinkable had already happened in our lives, and I was very much aware it could happen again.* I couldn't shake the fear that overtook me from this trauma trigger, even after we found him, pulled over to the side of the road, and he safely approached us.

I couldn't even speak to Seth. A tidal wave of emotions hit me violently all at once. I kicked and beat the dashboard and the inside door of the truck. I screamed and cried hysterically at the top of my lungs. I kept yelling, "Why? Why? Why?" I had been transported back to the nightmare that began on September 28th. I couldn't catch my breath, and I was out of control. I was scared out of my mind and angry. Seth saw how I was and could not figure out what was going on with his mother! His dad had to explain to him what I was going through. I didn't calm down until we were halfway home. When I could talk, I said, "Why would you do that when you *know* what could happen to you? You are *not* invincible! You may not die, but you can set yourself back with another injury. Don't you know that? Some things may not take your life but can take away your quality of life!" The whole scenario exhausted me. I said my piece, but I knew I had to get a grip moving forward.

When he came home from the hospital after the initial accident, we pushed hard for him to get his life back, but part of that involved releasing Seth. It was difficult to do because the risks were inevitable and still are. I knew I would have given my life to give him back his, and I felt I had done just that, but I couldn't keep giving at that level. I didn't have it in me. I had exhausted that. The suffocating anxiety that accompanied this commitment of releasing Seth and entrusting his life to God has been excruciating at times. But it was the necessary thing to do for Seth to gain independence. He could not be independent unless I let go. What do you need to release?

If you live your life always braced for the next bad thing to happen, it's like holding your breath and never exhaling. Eventually, you will stop breathing and stop living. Pain is part of life, and so is taking risks. You can live the rest of your days in the predictable shallows of life, always waiting for the tsunami to overtake you. Or, you can exhale and face your fears. Neither choice is easy, but I promise, the latter is better than the former.

Chapter 17

WHEN FEAR AND FAITH COLLIDE

*"Your world's not falling apart, it's falling into place,
I'm on the throne, stop holding on and just be held."*

— Lyrics of *Just Be Held* by Casting Crowns

After undergoing surgery on May 9, 2019, to stop the leakage of brain fluid we discovered while shaving his head, Seth spent several days in the hospital. Though his chance at training for the Paralympics was temporarily postponed, and he had to mourn that, he still had a burning passion for competing. He was ready to get back into training and move into his future. He wanted to continue pursuing his dreams of being on the USA Paralympic Team, and we supported him. Our family and friends were excited that his surgery was a success, and on June 27, 2019, he was officially released to begin training again. He felt ready to launch himself back into life.

Fast forward five days later. It was Tuesday, July 2, 2019, and Seth was driving his pick-up truck in our hometown. He had just left a friend visiting our area, a young girl he had met who was also a brain injury survivor. As he headed home, a woman driving an 18-wheeler took too wide of a turn and sideswiped Seth's truck. Out of all the ways he could have been injured, he hit his head on the driver's side window, smack dab on his recent graft. Upon impact, his skin graft popped open around the perimeter. Intense pain shot through his head, but he didn't lose consciousness.

In fact, Seth had the presence of mind to immediately call me on his cell phone. While in a full adrenaline rush, he conveyed what happened as best as he could. I clearly understood that the woman who had just hit him was fleeing the scene. As she fled, Seth followed her in his truck down the highway! He honked his horn repeatedly until she finally pulled over in the median. He pulled his vehicle directly behind her, and, as he did, a police officer showed up. When the woman figured out that Seth couldn't speak, she lied and told the officer that Seth was the one who hit her. All this happened close to home, and I was able to get to Seth as this conversation was underway. I let the officer know that the woman was lying and that the dash cam would prove it. When she heard me say "dash cam," she quickly shut her mouth! She knew she was guilty, and the more she talked, the more trouble she would incur.

Thankfully, we had done our due diligence in case anything like this ever happened. Our efforts doubled in keeping tabs on Seth once he was released to drive. For instance, we had a tracking device installed on his vehicle so our family would always know his location. Before Seth began driving on his own, I laminated a detailed note to keep in his glove box in case he was ever stopped by an officer. It explained his communication deficits and supplied the necessary contact information in case of an emergency. (He carried a similar note in his wallet along with a TBI identification card.) There was also a dash cam installed in his truck's rearview mirror. This device proved to be the most valuable in this case. The camera captured the moments before, during, and after the impact of the woman's 18-wheeler.

This accident set in motion yet another massive setback for Seth. We knew his skin graft had been compromised when it struck the window, but we assumed that it could be sutured (similar to stitching a hole in a garment). As it turned out, this surgery "patch job" would not be a one-and-done. We didn't know it then, but Seth would wind up with several issues due to the damage this latest accident inflicted on him. There would be many more doctor's appointments and hospital stays due to his run-in with the 18-wheeler. It would prove to be an ongoing collision in his life. He underwent two more extensive surgical revisions on that graft site (and had to have it stitched and cauterized several more times). For three years, he had to wear a large bandage around his head. You would think this would make him reluctant to go out in public. Not Seth! We used to joke that he looked like he stepped out of a war zone.

After numerous complications, he underwent months of daily specialized wound care in a hyperbaric chamber. Of course, such specialized treatment was not available in our area. This meant we had to make a three-hour round-trip drive every day. Despite all the surgeries and therapy, Seth's graft continued to leak, eventually leading to yet another major surgery down the road. Unbeknownst to us, there was more going on under the surface.

The fact that it happened mere weeks after Seth had been released was an enormous blow.

In the midst of all this, his dad and I were on the brink of disaster in our relationship. The turmoil in our marriage had been present for quite some time, but everything came to a head. Seth was left to deal with the heartache he felt over this situation while dealing with the pain and disappointment surrounding his own circumstances. It was a lot. In fact, it was too much.

The Slippery Slope of Despair

Once again, success is not a linear trek. It's a broken road where fear and faith wrestle. What do you do when your faith can't find the way? When your compass no longer works, and it feels like you're in spiritual vertigo, drowning in a dark abyss? When you can't see the light of day or hear the voice of your Savior?

I had to help Seth remember that everything he was going through did not come to stay; it came to pass. God was with him, and he would get through this. One day at a time. One moment at a time. One step at a time. He would make it to the other side. (This applies to you and whatever you're going through as well!) Keeping this in the forefront of Seth's mind was just a part of my role as his caregiver. He needed me to speak the truth, especially after this latest combination of setbacks.

Although I could speak the truth, I couldn't make it soak through to his heart. How could I place this hope inside of him that things would get better? Only God has the power to do that. Still, I was intentional about reminding my precious son of God's Biblical truths and promises. Now in his early twenties, he had been through unimaginable challenges but also had received much mercy. I prayed and asked others to pray. Seth prayed, too. And, let's get real, we felt angry sometimes, and we both shed lots of tears. Throughout it all, we knew we could trust God somehow with what we didn't understand. Seth needed to cling to faith so he would not slip into utter despair. So did I.

Pick Me Up Some Faith, Please!

As you know by now, this was not Seth's first rodeo with needing great faith. He had been clinging to his faith in God every day as he lived out his journey. One example that stands out to me and illustrates his understanding of his need for faith happened not long after we brought him home from the hospital, right before his eighteenth

> *Success is not a linear trek. It's a broken road where fear and faith wrestle.*

birthday. He had just begun speech therapy the day before, near our home at Louisiana Tech. We enrolled him in a program at the university where supervised graduate students would work directly with Seth on his speech. We felt especially good about this practical support because the students, their professor, and the director had an optimistic stance regarding Seth's needs that we liked.

It was important to surround Seth with a positive support

group that would encourage him to see past the many obstacles he faced. Those who stood out in his recovery process and had the most significant impact had been those with that same outlook. They added fuel to his spirit of determination by not only pointing to the mountain in front of Seth but acknowledging the big and small feats he accomplished in the process of ascending that mountain.

On his second day of speech therapy, we were allowed to observe Seth and the grad students working with him through a two-way mirror. (Another group of grad students was in the room with us so they could learn by observation.) We were thrilled to discover, as we watched and heard Seth, that he was making more clear sounds than ever before. After the session, the director and professor came in to talk with us, affirming that he did great. They spoke of his determination and how hard he was working. But they also said that because of those things, Seth would struggle with a heightened level of frustration. He sometimes felt defeated because his speech wasn't returning as quickly as he wanted it to. I didn't doubt their words, but I didn't expect the reality of them to hit Seth so soon.

Later that afternoon, once we returned home, his dad was getting ready to pick up some things at the store and asked, "Seth, you want me to bring you back anything?" Seth signed, "Yes," so his dad handed him a piece of paper and a pen to write down what he wanted. I know I would've written down something like "chips and salsa," so we were caught off guard when we saw what Seth wrote. On the paper, he had scrawled the word "FAITH."

You can imagine how I felt. I had been rejoicing over the wonderful therapy session at Louisiana Tech hours earlier, but Seth was struggling with it. He was frustrated, feeling defeated. It was difficult for us to hold back tears when our son was hurting so badly. Finally, his dad said, "Seth, I'll bring you back a book on faith." That's the best we could do for him. At that moment, I was reminded of the unimaginable daily struggle Seth was dealing with in his mind. I was experiencing my own constant struggle, trying to convince myself that everything would be all right.

As I spoke truth to myself, I passed it on to Seth. I reminded him, "You used to tell us your favorite scripture was Romans 8:28. You always said, 'It's all good.' Son, no matter what it feels like, you have to keep believing that God is working this out for your good because He is." I felt like a broken record at times, but I had to keep the truth in the forefront of his mind. (If only we could buy an extra-large container of faith at the store! Faith is available to all, but it can't be purchased, though that would make things simpler.)

For a while, that piece of paper stayed in my Bible to remind me that no matter what we are going through, we must never forget that the thing people need most in their difficult situations (and all their pain) is faith. Today, that paper hangs as a daily reminder in my curio cabinet, displayed for all to see. We all have days when we need more faith.

Grief Compounded

Fast forward several years to what he was going through now: deep sadness over missing out on the Paralympics, continued pain from the initial surgery to stop the brain fluid leak in addition to "fresh" pain from his latest accident, added trauma, and the stress and dread of knowing he'd have to get back onto the operating table at some point and take care of this latest injury. His physical pain was often debilitating, and his emotional pain overtook him like a tsunami. He was experiencing such overwhelming weariness from the physical, mental, and emotional fight he was in. It threatened to pull him down into a miry pit like never before.

To make matters worse, his grief over these latest events was compounded by his dad and I going through a divorce. The turmoil in our marriage had been going on for quite some time, but everything was coming to a head. His dad previously suffered a year-long mental breakdown. Now he was deeply enmeshed in another one. (It had been a traumatic and tumultuous time for years.) When his dad had his second mental breakdown and left, he took most of our savings. I could no longer plug the holes on this sinking ship, or we would all drown. Not everything can be salvaged. So, after years of giving our marriage all I could, we proceeded with divorce. While dealing with his pain, disappointments, and emotions surrounding his circumstances, Seth also had to wrestle with this heartbreaking reality. His dad's poor choices, coupled with his mental illness, severed our family. It devastated all of us.

Trauma happens to the family unit as a whole. His mental

breakdown was partly due to how he dealt (or rather didn't) with Seth's accident years before. He needed to seek professional help, but he didn't take the steps necessary to receive it and work toward recovery. Ironically, though Seth suffered emotionally from the divorce, he was a significant support to me during this time. Amid his heartache, Seth ministered to me. Despite his limited vocabulary, I clearly understood the message. I had always been the encourager, the motivator, and the coach for him. Now he was that for me.

I was a wreck during the divorce and in my own dark place, but Seth continued to encourage me. His tenderness was like a healing balm. I saw how it ministered to him as he ministered to me. (Remember that Booker T. Washington quote? "If you want to lift yourself up, lift up someone else.") After the divorce was final, Seth pushed me to make a list of things I would want in a husband. He told me to be specific, right down to eye color and build! It took me some time, but I finally wrote the list to shut Seth up. (Seth is always persistent). I thought I did it to appease my son, but you know what? I found that it was therapeutic for me! Doing this enabled me to move on. (Seth was well-educated in the list-making-for-a-mate department. He had made his years ago and still has it on his phone, praying over the list as he waits for "the one.") Then, Seth told me to write a list of qualities I have to offer a new husband. This part of the assignment stumped me. I began to cry because I couldn't think of one thing! I was deeply hurt over the past, and some things my ex-husband was doing poured salt on my wounds, making things that much harder. Still, Seth wouldn't let me off the hook. He began to tell me the qualities I had that would be a gift to a future husband. He made me write them down and helped me believe them! Seth was there for me in my dark days while in the midst of his own.

During all this, I believe there was another ongoing issue that added to Seth's grief. It had to do with his relationships outside of our family. A reality that accompanied Seth's traumatic brain injury was his difficulty experiencing and enjoying lasting, deep friendships. The tight friendships he enjoyed before September 28, 2011, did not continue after that date. To this day, most people are polite and sincerely interested in Seth—for a time. But after a while, they grow tired of how challenging it is to carry on a conversation with him. They have to listen actively and creatively. People become weary of texting, which is an effective way for Seth to communicate but tiresome after a while. It takes a good measure of effort, patience, and time to be in a relationship with Seth—more than most people are willing to give. He has some people in his life who have fulfilled this desire to a degree, but he craves ongoing, meaningful relationships with his peers. He desires to be in a relationship with a woman, but being unable to date or communicate as most people are used to is a significant hurdle. (He did have a girlfriend for a while, but their relationship ended after about two years.)

Along with having fun and being silly, Seth has always enjoyed debating and discussing in-depth issues. Finding people who will stick around for the long haul and engage in this way with him has been a challenge. It takes a special person to be with a special person. The truth is, he was lonely.

Seth had only been cleared to drive again about a month

before his run-in with the 18-wheeler. For that month, he could taste some independence and enjoy driving himself to the gym, Walmart, or wherever he felt like going. He loved this newfound freedom. Seth, a grown man now, was tired of being dependent on other family members and me. To make matters worse, after the accident with the 18-wheeler and after his dad left, Seth started having seizures and could no longer drive. The seizures were a new development that was both scary and discouraging. They also further added to the number of his medical appointments and my ever-growing anger and grief. I fought hard to maintain a positive attitude and atmosphere since stress can trigger seizures. I also had to be extra diligent to help Seth keep on top of things at this point, and he quickly became fed up with having to hear me say, "Don't lift that!" "Don't eat that!" "Don't do that!" And I don't blame him. It was all so depressing. And it went on for quite some time.

The Battle is First Won in Your Mind

This latest accident (and all that came with it) began a downward spiral leading Seth into his most grim moments. A dark vortex developed from the recovery battle he had fought for so many years (and from all the setbacks he suffered along the way). The physical and emotional pain from the latest accident added to his trauma. He was sucked down to another dimension of darkness that he couldn't think or pray his way out of. His faith didn't seem to be enough. His grief and pain were intense. He contemplated suicide.

As best as I can understand and explain, what Seth was experiencing was like being in a cave. When my kids were young, we went on a family trip to Mammoth Cave National Park in Kentucky. While we were there, we joined in on a cave tour. Lights installed inside the cave lit the way for us to explore, but at one point, the guide had us stand still and look at our hands. He told us that he would turn out the lights and when he did, we would experience "absolute darkness." Even though my hand was right in front of my face, I couldn't see anything because there wasn't a speck of light. It was also eerie to have a sense of *feeling* darkness. This was what Seth was experiencing emotionally. With all that was currently upon him, he couldn't imagine that things would ever get better. He felt as if what his life was at that moment was all it would ever be. I knew if he sat with those thoughts long enough, they would feed into his spirit and wreak havoc unto death. Like water torture, those thoughts would become a *drip, drip, drip* on his psyche and do irreparable damage. Thankfully, amid these awful moments that sometimes turned into days, a ray of light would shine through. That tiny sliver would be enough to let some hope in. In those moments, I could scrape him off the floor and help him refocus by gently (but with all the bold enthusiasm I could muster) speaking words of encouragement.

One thing I learned to do is to open his TikTok, Instagram, or his Facebook page and read him the different messages people sent. These words from strangers have served as fresh reminders that Seth's story has given people hope. They've written messages like, "I was an atheist, but you've helped me believe in God. I know your relationship with Him is real, and I want it, too." "I never used to pray, but now I do." "I decided not to commit suicide because if you're going through what you're going through, I can hang in there despite my issues." "Because of you, I got out of bed today." These messages from all over the world have been a significant encouragement to Seth over the years.

Satan has obviously wanted him to lose the battle and give up, but time and time again, God provided encouragement that helped Seth get back into the right frame of mind and trust once again. He has often been asked on TikTok how he gets through his many challenges. His answer is always the same: He points to his head and says, "Mind. Up, up, up." This is his way of telling people that battles are first won in the mind before they're ever fought on the battlefield. Satan wants to mess with our psyche. The mind is a muscle to be disciplined. Listening to what God has to say and ignoring the enemy's lies is essential to a strong, emotionally healthy mind. Thankfully, even on the darkest days, Seth has been able to embrace this truth and move toward it. Just one small step toward truth makes an essential difference.

Seth had (and continues to have) two choices: He could cling to Romans 8:28 and believe God's Word to be the truth, or he could abandon his faith (or, at the very least, become numb to it). Many have done just that over circumstances much less traumatic than Seth's. For years, he started each morning with Romans 8:28 (NIV) on his lips: *And we know that in all things, God works for the good of those who love him, who are called according to his purpose."* But did he *really* believe them? He was being tested, it seemed, yet again. Thankfully, Seth chose to hold fast to God's Word. If he had abandoned his faith and the unwavering truth of God's Word, I have no doubt his despair would have taken him down completely. God was also able to continue to use Seth in my life and many others, even though he was hurting. Life often seems unfair like this, but when we surrender our hurts and disappointments to the Lover of Our Soul, He uses us and sustains us for His purposes and our good. He remains with us all the while, never leaving or forsaking us.

Having to battle depression has ebbed and flowed over the years, but Seth continues to fight when he needs to. When he has experienced a significant setback and felt the weariness of the battle to his core, he has longed at times for his heavenly home, where there will be no more tears, pain, and heartache.

One day (following the 18-wheeler accident), Seth said, "Mom, I miss heaven. I miss Jesus. I want to go back there." That was hard to hear, but I couldn't blame him. Not only that, I understood. Years earlier, he had shared something with me with which I was already familiar. Seth told me about his encounter with Jesus when he died at the accident scene and while he was in a coma. I understood what he was experiencing at the time because the Lord had miraculously let me in on it. God spoke to my heart and showed me with my own eyes.

Chapter 18

MOM, I MET JESUS!

"He that dwelleth in the secret place of the most High shall
abide under the shadow of the Almighty.
I will say of the Lord, He is my refuge and my fortress: my
God; in him will I trust.
Surely he shall deliver thee from the snare of the fowler,
and from the noisome pestilence.
He shall cover thee with his feathers, and under his wings
shalt thou trust: his truth shall be thy shield and buckler.
Thou shalt not be afraid for the terror by night; nor for the
arrow that flieth by day;
Nor for the pestilence that walketh in darkness; nor for the
destruction that wasteth at noonday."

— Psalm 91:1-6 (KJV)

The morning after Seth had been airlifted to the trauma center, I remember briefly leaving so I could get cleaned up before the next ICU visitation. I sat in my tub, still reeling, longing to wake from this hellish nightmare. I screamed and cried out through my tears, "God, where are you? Why did you let this happen to my son?" I tried to wrap my head around the awful events that had transpired and somehow find a reason for it all. At that moment, a still, small voice spoke to my heart and said, "I have him in my Secret Place."

The Secret Place

Then I saw it! God showed me a vision of the most beautiful field of wildflowers and gently rolling hills. It was a perfect, serene Spring day—the kind only seen in your sweetest dreams. The sky was a vibrant Caribbean blue that even the most picturesque ocean couldn't rival. Hummingbirds and butterflies danced from flower to flower. The birds sang the most delightful melody as the wind filled the atmosphere with a pleasant aroma. It was as if all of nature was whispering a symphony of praise. As I sat in my tub, peace and tranquility washed over me like a gentle rain. The Bible talks about having peace that passes understanding, but this was the first time I had ever experienced it for myself.

It was then that I heard it: the unmistakable sound of my son's laughter. My eyes were drawn toward the sound of his deep, boisterous laugh. In the distance stood a majestic oak tree, its branches stretched wide, offering the perfect shade. There he was! Seth was sitting on the ground beneath this magnificent oak. His legs were outstretched with his ankles crossed, but he wasn't alone. Though I had never seen Him before, my heart immediately recognized the man sitting beside him. It was Jesus!

They looked like two close friends laughing and talking with one another. Though I couldn't make out what they were saying, there were points in the conversation when Jesus would turn and whisper something to Seth. Seth's expression would change as he listened intently to what Jesus was saying. Then the sound would grow louder as they began talking and laughing again. I didn't want this scene before me to disappear. Though it was brief, I was deeply grateful for it.

The following day I shared with my family the vision God had shown me, but I never mentioned it to Seth. Several months after Seth came home from the hospital, he shared with us what happened when he died. He said, "Jesus…Me…best, best friends…close, close, close. Funny"

What Was Jesus Like?

Seth's eyes lit up as he described Jesus. Through his limited words, charades, drawing pictures, and showing images off the internet, Seth told us that Jesus was about 6'2" with dark hair and a dark beard. He had piercing blue eyes that were so full of light they looked as if they were on fire. Seth said Christ did not look weak and effeminate like the paintings and figurines we see prominently displayed. Instead, he said Jesus was muscular and strong, much like you would assume a carpenter would be.

Seth described the place where he met Jesus and called it *His Secret Place.* It was the same as what I saw in the vision months ago, but with much more detail!

Manna and Honey

Seth said he and Jesus walked along a cobblestone path inlaid with diamonds and gold stones of different shapes and sizes. The stones were so pure you could see your reflection in them like a mirror. There was no sun and no clouds in the beautiful expanse of sky. There was no need for either in this perfect biosphere. Christ was the light.

They continued on the path, surrounded on either side by perfectly manicured emerald-green grass, until they came to a magnificent fountain nestled between two large trees. It was approximately twenty feet high, with a thin, honey-like substance flowing down multiple tiers and into a large, pool-like basin. The basin was broad enough that it offered seating all the way around. They sat down, and Jesus leaned over, dipped his hand into the pool of honey-like substance, and took a drink. He encouraged Seth to do the same. Seth said he had never tasted anything so sweet and satisfying.

Then Jesus told Seth that he had to go back because he had a great purpose yet to fulfill. Seth said there was such happiness in that place words could not describe, and he didn't want to leave. Before He sent Seth back, Jesus told him that he would speak again and that when it was time, he would speak the words Christ had given him.

What Lies Behind the Veil

"For now, we see but a faint reflection of riddles and mysteries as though reflected in a mirror, but one day we will see face-to-face. My understanding is incomplete now, but one day I will understand everything, just as everything about me has been fully understood."

— 1 Corinthians 13:12 (TPT)

The unknown is always unsettling to us humans. For those of us who have not stepped behind the Veil, it can be fearful and hard to comprehend. Since that day, Seth's response to someone passing away has been different. Instead of sadness, Seth is filled with joy and excitement for the person. Why? He said they get to meet Jesus and experience the joy and peace of His presence forever. Of course, the selfish part of our humanity wants to physically hold on tightly to those we care about and love. So, we can only perceive it as our loss. But my whole perception of life after death has changed. We can feel God's presence when we worship, but can you imagine being in His tangible, physical presence 24/7? Imagine touching Jesus! Looking into His eyes and seeing Him face-to-face! I can see why Seth rejoices when someone passes away. It truly is a day of celebration to think they are forever experiencing the joy and peace of His presence.

When you think of it from that perspective, it's very peaceful. How reassuring to know this is not our final resting place. One day we will be where there is no more sadness and no more tears. Fear and depression will not exist, only happiness as we've never known here.

We know there is a greater life after this life. None of us will live forever on this side of the Veil, but on the other side, we will have eternal life. There's a life far greater for you if you have invited Christ to be the Lord of your life. There is a Savior who gave everything for you so you can live your life with purpose. There is more He wants to show you. Just open your heart and let Him come in.

Would You Like to Follow Jesus? Here's Your Invitation:

There is not a person on earth who doesn't find themselves in a dark place at some point. When we are questioning, hurting, or feeling lost, we need some light, the kind that brings direction, healing, hope, vision, and comfort. Jesus said, "I am light to the world, and those who embrace me will experience life-giving light, and they will never walk in darkness" (John 8:12 TPT). Without the light and love of Jesus, this world is a profoundly dark place, and we are lost forever.

Jesus, in His great love, wants us to look to Him, and when we do, light penetrates the darkness. As we respond to the love of Jesus, our hearts are unlocked to see more of his beauty and glory. When we look to Him, we see ourselves and our lives differently. Our perspective changes, and we understand that Jesus doesn't define us by our failures but by His love for us. When we take one step toward Jesus, He meets us and begins His work in our lives. When that happens, our hearts begin to open to the precious discovery of the wonder of Jesus Christ.

Everything recorded in the Bible is there so that you will fully believe that Jesus is the Son of God and that through your faith in Him, you will experience eternal life by the power of his name (see John 20:31).

If you long for this light and love in your life, say a prayer like this—whether for the first time or to start again and reignite your desire to follow Jesus:

Jesus, You are the light of the world. I want to follow You fervently and wholeheartedly. I know my sins have separated me from You, but still, You love me. I'm so grateful! Thank You for paying the price for my sins. I trust Your finished work on the cross for my rescue. I turn away from the thoughts and deeds that have separated me from You. Please forgive me and awaken me to love You with all my heart, mind, soul, and strength. I believe God raised You from the dead, and I want that new life to flow through me each day and for eternity. God, I willingly give You my life and trust You to lead and guide me. Now fill me with Your Spirit so that my life will honor You, and I will be equipped to fulfill Your purpose for me. Amen.

You can be confident that what Jesus said about those who choose to follow Him is true: "If you embrace my message and believe in the One who sent me, you will never face condemnation, for in me, you have already passed from the realm of death into the realm of eternal life!" (John 5:24 TPT). But that's not all! You are declared "not guilty" by God because of Jesus, and you are also considered his most intimate friend (John 15:15).

As you grow in your relationship with Jesus, continue to read the Bible, talk to God through prayer, spend time with others who follow Jesus, and live out your faith daily and passionately. You have favor with God; He will bless you and never leave you!

At no time during this journey have we ever been ashamed or apologetic about our faith. We've never hidden that it has been what has carried us through. There were many times our fear and our faith would wrestle. In the end, our faith would win. Through the many cycles of setbacks and comebacks, we have remained truthful about where we stand with Jesus whenever we share our story with people. Have we felt anger, despair, and discouragement at times? Absolutely! Yet both of us have a genuine and intimate relationship with God that will never be extinguished due to any kind of circumstances. God is well aware of our feelings and invites us to be honest with Him. So, if you're a believer or thinking of becoming one, please know that God never expects you to put on a happy face and not allow your feelings to affect you. He knows you thoroughly and made you who you are: a physical, spiritual, *and* emotional human being! He can handle your anger, tears, and doubts. He can handle your temper tantrums and seasons of being tempted to walk away and give up. But because of His great love for you,

> *The presence of grief doesn't mean the absence of faith. Grief is an integral part of healing.*

He continues to journey with you no matter what. He is an ever-present help in times of need. God desires a close relationship with you. He wants you to praise Him for the good and tell Him everything you're worried about. He wants to walk with you through every part of your life—the good, the bad, and the ugly. He cares deeply for you. Yes, He knows everything before you tell Him. But, He wants to hear your voice and for you to hear His. You may ask, "How can I hear His voice?"

Through His Word. Take Philippians 4:6-7 (TPT), for example. Let it soak in and allow it to speak to your heart: *"Don't be pulled in different directions or worried about a thing. Be saturated in prayer throughout each day, offering your faith-filled requests before God with overflowing gratitude. Tell him every detail of your life, then God's wonderful peace that transcends human understanding will guard your heart and mind through Jesus Christ."* Amen!

God also accepts your praise. Sometimes you may offer it sacrificially, meaning you don't *feel* like praising Him, but you do it anyway because you believe He is worthy. Praising Him even though you don't understand the "why" to whatever is going on in your life pleases Him. Offering God praise—which is acknowledging who He is—even when He doesn't come through like you thought He should or hoped He would, is God-honoring and, believe it or not, will encourage you. When we praise Him during difficult circumstances as well as joyful ones, our faith deepens. It matures. Our love for Him grows. I've seen that in Seth's life and experienced it in my own life.

We've also experienced grief. The presence of grief doesn't mean the absence of faith. Grief is an integral part of healing; we've learned quite a bit about it over the years. It's important to grieve and trust God as you walk through the process.

Chapter 19

THE CYCLE OF GRIEF

*"We bereaved are not alone. We belong to the largest
company in all the world—the company of those
who have known suffering."*

— Helen Keller

Part of walking into the future is letting go of the past. Our lives were forever changed when Seth was hit by the van while riding his bike. He was a different person. I had to grieve the loss of who he was before I could move forward. People often think of grief as lasting weeks or months. The reality is that it may take years.

The grieving process cannot be forced or rushed, and there is no one-size-fits-all. Everyone experiences grief differently. No matter your situation and depth of grief, be patient with yourself. You may experience all five stages, only to repeat the cycle again and again.

Imagine the grieving process as a funnel. At the beginning of the process, visualize yourself at the widest part of the funnel. When you're at this point, it takes longer to process through each stage of grief. Just as a funnel narrows as it nears the bottom, the difficult periods become shorter and less intense as time goes by. As the cycle repeats, don't expect to experience the stages in neat, sequential order. You may even find yourself spending more time vacillating between two stages. Even years later, a strong sense of grief may be triggered unexpectedly by a song, a season, or a familiar scent. Don't worry about what stage you should be in or what you're supposed to be feeling. Allow yourself to move through the process naturally.

Another thing I learned is that men and women tend to grieve differently. In our case, my (ex) husband was a strong, alpha-male type. He was never one to cry or show weakness. But as we journeyed with Seth through all that was happening, that changed. He began to cry frequently and needed a great deal of encouragement from me. I was trying to keep myself strong for Seth. Though he shed many tears, I don't believe my ex walked successfully through the necessary steps and truly grieved. As a result, his mind eventually broke under the weight of it all.

What I discovered about myself during this time is that a significant component of how I handle grief is staying busy. Working to turn Seth's story into ministry somehow was extremely helpful to me. Starting the Team Seth Foundation for those suffering from a traumatic brain injury brought something positive—a true purpose—to my pain and helped me to move through it.

On top of everything going on with Seth, the end of my marriage compounded my grief. It's not uncommon for marriages to suffer and ultimately end when the couple is to fulfill the role of caregiver for someone with an acquired disability. I believe Seth's dad and I would have done better had we gone through grief counseling, individually and as a couple. Both of us would have had to show up for that, however.

There are times the cycle of grief feels more like a never-ending whirlpool. Do you feel helpless and isolated in the middle of the ocean? Are you buffeted by stormy waves on all sides? Is it hard for you to breathe with the crushing weight on your lungs? Do you gasp for air as your head breaks the surface only to be immediately sucked back under? If so, reach out for help! Don't drown when a life preserver is within arm's reach. The last thing you need to do is "go it alone." There are some things that are so complex that you can't navigate them by yourself. Grief is one of those things. I can't say it enough: Find a grief counselor or a therapist who is trained to help you!

The Five Stages[4]

1. Denial

Driving home that afternoon on September 28, 2011, after celebrating my birthday by retreating to our cabin in the Arkansas mountains, I could never have imagined the phone call I would receive. Picking up the phone to be greeted by a hysterical Sierrah could never have been predicted. When this news was relayed to me, my first thought was, *This can't be happening. He's okay. It's not as severe as they think.*

When we finally reached the trauma center, the neuro-surgeon informed us that the next 48 hours were critical, and

---

4 Kübler-Ross, Elisabeth. *On Death and Dying.* Scribner, 1969.

they did not expect Seth to survive. I could not wrap my head around what he was saying. I was numb and in a state of shock. Was this really happening? I desperately tried to wake myself from this nightmare, only to realize I wasn't asleep.

Though your brain is aware of what is happening around you, it cannot initially process such traumatic information. Experiencing denial was a surreal experience. Have you ever watched a movie where someone is beheaded? You know, that gruesome scene where the executioner holds up the head and turns it around so the person can see their own detached body? That's an apt description of how I felt. I could not believe what I was hearing and seeing. For anyone in grief experiencing denial, it's not until after the initial shock subsides that your brain can begin to process the trauma and loss.

2. Anger

I experienced a plethora of anger as a result of Seth's injury. I was angry at the woman who hit him. I was outraged that she only received a ticket and drove to get her van fixed the next day. I was furious that she never reached out to us and showed no concern. I remember thinking, *If I had hit someone's dog, I would've had the common decency to stop and apologize for the accident!* It wasn't until many years later that we found out the woman's insurance company had advised her and her adult son not to reach out to us. By that time, I had already demonized this woman in my mind.

I was also angry at family members who had a close relationship with Seth before his brain injury and were suddenly nowhere to be found. I was mad at his friends for deserting him in his darkest hour (after he stood beside them during theirs).

I was even angry with Seth. We had told him long before his accident that we didn't want him riding on that stretch of the road and reminded him of that again as we left. He waited until I was out of town and then chose that route for his bike ride. How could he disobey me like that? Why didn't he listen?

And yes, as I've previously mentioned, I was angry at God.

I tried to suppress my anger, but I was like a volcano, always simmering beneath the surface, boiling on the inside, and ready to erupt. Anger spread like cancer inside of me. It distorted my view of everything. I couldn't see anything beautiful for a time— only the narrative I had constructed with poisoned ink.

My anger scared me. I saw a part of myself that I didn't know existed. Curses now seemed to be always on the tip of my tongue. I felt like a fraud as a co-pastor walking into church on Sundays. Here I was, trying to encourage people in our congregation when I wasn't sure if I believed anymore. Anger affects your judgment. It causes you to look at people through a jaded lens. Trauma mixed with anger equals disillusionment with everyone and everything around you.

You cannot avoid anger. You have to go through it. The more you allow yourself to truly feel anger, the more it will begin to dissipate. I didn't find healing until I got real with others and shared my struggle. It's scary to make yourself vulnerable and transparent, but I discovered I wasn't such a bad person after all. I found out I wasn't alone. More importantly, I realized that, like my pain, there could be a purpose in my anger if I chose to use my experience to bring hope and healing to someone else.

3. Bargaining

I begged God as I tried to negotiate for Seth's life and pleaded with him to let me trade places...

My life for his.
Put his pain on me instead.
Just please spare my son's life. I'll do anything.

Guilt is a part of the bargaining stage because your mind tries to rationalize things that are not rational. Irrational guilt will haunt you if left unchecked. I found myself reliving the moments leading up to Seth's accident. I replayed every word spoken and regretted every word left unsaid. If only I would have said this or done that, my son wouldn't be lying in a coma and fighting for his life.

For years after the accident, Seth's dad struggled with guilt for buying Seth a bicycle and for introducing him to cycling in the first place. I struggled with being out of town when the accident occurred.

Guilt is often mistaken for grief. When you're grieving, it's easy to confuse the two. How do you tell the difference? Guilt is what you feel when you've done something immoral or evil. It's almost always the direct result of an action that could have been avoided, while grief results from an uncontrollable circumstance. Grief is a natural response to loss.

4. Depression

Depression is fueled by regret. Trauma and loss often result in depression. During this stage, I grieved deeper than

I could have ever imagined, and it felt like it would never end. Remember how I said you might not experience the stages of grief in sequential order? It's also possible to experience more than one stage simultaneously. For me, anger and depression hit at the same time.

I remember logging onto Facebook to update his Team Seth page only to be confronted with a post from one of his former college classmates. She was excited about graduating from nursing school, and I became so angry. While his classmates were celebrating receiving their diplomas, we celebrated Seth learning to write his name again. This was the day that was supposed to usher in the next chapter of his life. He was supposed to begin his career as a travel nurse and see the world! The mile marker that was supposed to propel him into his dream mocked me. It was a looming reminder of everything he had lost...everything we had lost. I wasn't just angry; I was overwhelmed with despair and hopelessness. How could everybody just forget? How could everyone keep going on with their lives while Seth had lost his completely? I felt like he had gotten left behind, and it wasn't fair. The world just kept spinning.

Before the accident, Seth was so outgoing. He loved debating and holding deep, intellectual discussions. For a long time after his accident, he couldn't even communicate one sentence. He couldn't write. He couldn't text. He couldn't read. He even had difficulty processing and comprehending what other people were saying. It was like he was locked in a glass box—he knew what he wanted to say, but there was no way to get it out.

It wasn't just his nursing class who had moved on, but everyone else in his life, too. He had cousins his age starting their careers and getting married, and Seth couldn't even bathe or dress himself. It was then that the loss fully settled in my soul that the Seth I knew was not coming back. The sad realization that life, as you knew it was gone forever, is understandably depressing. When you're well aware of your present reality, it's hard to have a vision for your future.

If you can relate to any of this, let me warn you: When you're unable to focus past the limitations of your present circumstance, you will get stuck in depression. You may even find yourself withdrawing from life in a fog of intense sadness, wondering if there is any point in going on. Depression is not something you can just snap out of. It is a normal and appropriate response to trauma and loss. Depression is a necessary step along your journey to healing, but again, reach out for help as you move through it—for your sake and others. For example, if you have other children in your care, they can feel neglected and become resentful. Depression affects the whole family, so do what you can to heal and move past it.

5. Acceptance

The only pathway to peace is through surrender and acceptance. It took me a long time to get to this point. Accepting your new reality does not mean you're okay with what happened. Instead, you choose to focus on the future and not the past. You cannot replace what was lost, but you can make new memories, build a new life, and forge a new path.

Stop wishing for everything to go back to how it used to be and accept that loss has changed your life. Surrender your wants, your anger, your sadness, your disappointment. Begin to live again, and don't feel guilty about moving on and learning to smile again. You're not betraying what was by accepting what is.

In addition to seeking support from a grief counselor and/or becoming part of a grief support group, it helps to get outside your current environment. Exercise is a great way to feel good. Engaging in physical activity releases endorphins that trigger positive feelings. Go for a thirty-minute walk. For a bonus, walk outside! Sunshine boosts your serotonin which helps improve your mood. Exercise helps you refocus and refresh your mind and body. Learn a new skill. Explore new interests like yoga, cooking, and art—the possibilities are endless! You may be tempted, but do not self-medicate with alcohol or drugs to escape the pain. This will lead you down into an even darker pit. And whatever you do, don't quit moving forward in your life. Keep pushing through!

Chapter 20

"GOD, HELP ME FORGIVE" (THE PRISON OF UNFORGIVENESS)

"We cannot embrace God's forgiveness if we are so busy clinging to past wounds and nursing old grudges."

— T.D. Jakes

July 15, 2017. That's the morning God woke me up to write the words that have become the chapter you are now reading…

When something tragic happens to someone you love, you immediately start to assign blame. Especially when it was a senseless accident. Your mind tries to bring reason or justice to this horrible situation. It becomes your focal point—the person you can blame and direct all of your pain onto.

In the days, weeks, months, and even the first few years following Seth's accident, I was filled with powerful emotions toward the woman who ran over him. The complex blend of feelings I experienced would never come alone. They were always accompanied by another, compounding their effect. Buried beneath waves of bitterness and hate towards her, my emotions would erratically swing from one extreme to another. Out of nowhere, the force of emotion would catch me off guard as it washed over me like a tidal wave.

I could be sitting at a red light or standing in the grocery store and suddenly find myself weeping uncontrollably. I was overwhelmed by grief and sadness, and in the next moment, sheer gratitude would flood my soul. The joy of the present gift of my son's second chance at life was being eclipsed by my anger and my bitterness toward her. I could feel myself being buried alive beneath the weight of the negative emotions rooted in unforgiveness.

> *Unforgiveness will poison you from the inside out if you only see from a perspective of pain.*

There was really no one at fault. The accident hadn't been maliciously planned out. It was simply just that—an accident. I'm certain the elderly woman driving the van that hit my son had wished she could roll back time as much as I did. I'm sure she would have avoided my son altogether that day. None of us have the power to reverse the clock. We can only choose to make the best of what we have been given today.

Ironically, it was Seth's attitude that began to convict me and lead me out of my dark despair. He was the one who had every right to be full of anger, but he wasn't. He was the one whose plans for his life had been brought to a screeching halt. He was the one who had to live with a brain injury. He should have been full of bitterness and hate, but he wasn't! Instead, he was happy and grateful to be alive. So, how could I justify my struggle with forgiving her?

Seth had asked several times over the years to meet her,

and I had refused. I didn't want to face her. To add to my anger was the fact that the next day, while we sat in the ICU with our son, fighting for his life, she drove her van to a body shop to repair the damage from hitting my son. We were in the hospital for five months and never received a phone call from her or her family. There were no cards or flowers. There were no casseroles and no signs of remorse or compassion—only silence. In that space of silence, I found that the enemy is skilled at filling in the blanks for you. Like a prosecuting attorney, he builds a case against them to justify the prison of hate you have created.

Left unchecked, unforgiveness will poison you from the inside out. If you only see from a perspective of pain, it will skew your vision and spoil the beauty of the many blessings you have been given. Forgiveness is not saying that what someone did to hurt you was okay. It is simply leaving the judgment of that person up to God. My unforgiveness did not punish her. It did not take away one minute of her life, but it did mine.

I felt God telling me that my unforgiveness was holding me captive, and He wanted me to be fully free. I was reminded of Mark 11:25-26 (NKJV), *"And whenever you stand praying, if you have anything against anyone, forgive him, that your Father in heaven may also forgive you your trespasses. But if you do not forgive, neither will your Father in heaven forgive your trespasses."*

I knew I needed to be free, and I knew I could not do it alone. I needed God Almighty's help to unlock the chains that had me bound. I began to pray that God would help me to forgive and let go. I realized I had moved on to the next phase of forgiveness when I started to pray that she would find peace. You know you are truly free when you pray for God to bless the one you once prayed He would punish.

Over the years, the bitterness and hate toward her waned. The resentment was replaced by acceptance of my 'new norm' of caring for a son with a brain injury. Some moments would still catch me off-guard, but it was different. My feelings about her no longer consumed me. The tsunami of anger that would once overtake me had become more like a rolling wave in the shallows of the ocean. It would momentarily knock me off balance, but I would quickly regain my footing as I learned to release it back to God.

An Appointment With Destiny

July 15, 2017, was also the day God spoke to me and said, "Today is the day I want you and Seth to meet the woman that ran over him. I'm sending you to give her peace." As I sat at my keyboard typing, I wept. I did not want to face this woman. I had forgiven her. Wasn't that enough? No, God wanted her to know that we had. This was a spiritual boundary I would have to reluctantly but obediently cross.

I didn't know how to get in touch with her, so I messaged the woman's son on Facebook. As I hit "send," I thought, *Okay, God, I did my part.* However, I never thought I would receive a response, especially so quickly! Within ten minutes, he messaged me back. I told him we would like to meet his mother, and Seth wanted to pray for her. Our purpose in coming was to give her peace. Her family warned us that we might change our minds about wanting to meet her because she was in the latter stages of Alzheimer's and was incoherent most of the time. I knew I had to trust God and obey what He had told me to do.

To get to her house, we had to drive over the same bridge Seth was riding across when he was run over. He took out his phone and showed me four words God had given him: "Love, Hope, Peace & Grace." I remember telling Seth he was pretty amazing to be so full of God's love, and he replied, like always, "ALL GOD. Only God."

When we pulled into her driveway, I didn't think I would be able to get out of the car. I started crying. I couldn't do this. I could barely breathe! Recognizing that I was having a panic attack, Seth took my hand and said, "Mom, breathe." I couldn't. He said again, "Mom, look at me. Breathe." I locked eyes with him, and he took me through a deep breathing exercise. As I began to calm down, he reiterated, "Mom, trust God. All God."

After we knocked on her door, we were invited in and ushered into the living room. My eyes were immediately drawn to the elderly lady sitting in a recliner. She could have easily been anyone's sweet grandmother. Her snowy white hair was combed neatly around her face. She had gentle eyes and a kind smile, nothing at all like the monster I had imagined. The enemy had done a great job of painting a picture of her as a cold-hearted, old woman who did not care about the pain she had caused my family or the pain my son had endured. It was all a lie.

It was apparent that she was fully incapacitated and required 24/7 care. I didn't feel vindicated that she had to endure what Seth went through. Surprisingly, I didn't even feel hate or bitterness. I was filled with compassion, not only for her, but for her son and daughter-in-law. I was all too familiar with the burden they now carried as full-time caregivers.

Her daughter-in-law spoke first and introduced Seth. "Grandma, this is the young boy--well, now he is a young man--" She paused for a second and continued, "Nearly six years ago, he was riding his bike, and you accidentally hit him, and he almost died."

I corrected her and said, "No, ma'am, he actually *did* die twice at the scene. They also didn't expect him to live through the night. We were in the hospital for five months. Seth came home in a wheelchair and diapers and had to relearn everything."

The elderly lady turned to Seth with a troubled look on her face and said, "Oh, I am so, so sorry."

Seth took her hand and said, "Fine. Look at me! Strong! All God."

Watching my son comfort the woman who ran over him not only convicted me, it altered me. It's one thing to write about forgiveness. It's another thing to see it in action at that level.

The woman's son wept as he shared how tormented his mother had been by that fateful day. He said she would sit for hours and say, "I just didn't see him. I don't know what happened." And then she would pray, "God, please heal him and help him fully recover." He told us she was never the same after running over Seth and began to lose her mind shortly after.

I turned to her and said, "I want you to know that good has come out of this." I told her that from our tragedy, something beautiful happened. Not only did we see our weaknesses, but we also found our strengths. I shared about the Team Seth Foundation for Traumatic Brain Injury Awareness, our 501c3 that allowed us to assist many children with medical and therapy expenses.

She listened intently about how many people in their own impossible situations had discovered Seth's videos on YouTube and found the hope they so desperately needed. Because of what happened, Seth was able to preach the Gospel to more people without words than he could have ever reached before. People we would never have met otherwise had been saved, healed, and delivered. People who had never believed in the power of prayer were now believers in Christ!

I shared how I became an advocate for people with disabilities because of what I learned about advocating for my son. I told her I had become the Area Team Management Director for Special Olympics of Louisiana. I told her we shared our story about overcoming limitations and helping people push their pain into power on many platforms. I told her *none* of that would have occurred if Seth's accident had never happened.

How Do I Let Go?

Before we left, I said, "I want you to know God sent us here today to give you peace, and Seth would like to pray for you. Would that be okay?"

She smiled and sweetly said, "I love to pray." Her family gave me permission to video, but I will tell you there is no way to capture the feeling in that room as Seth prayed for her to have peace. Then he leaned over and kissed her on her forehead. I am thankful I was obedient because God knew that would

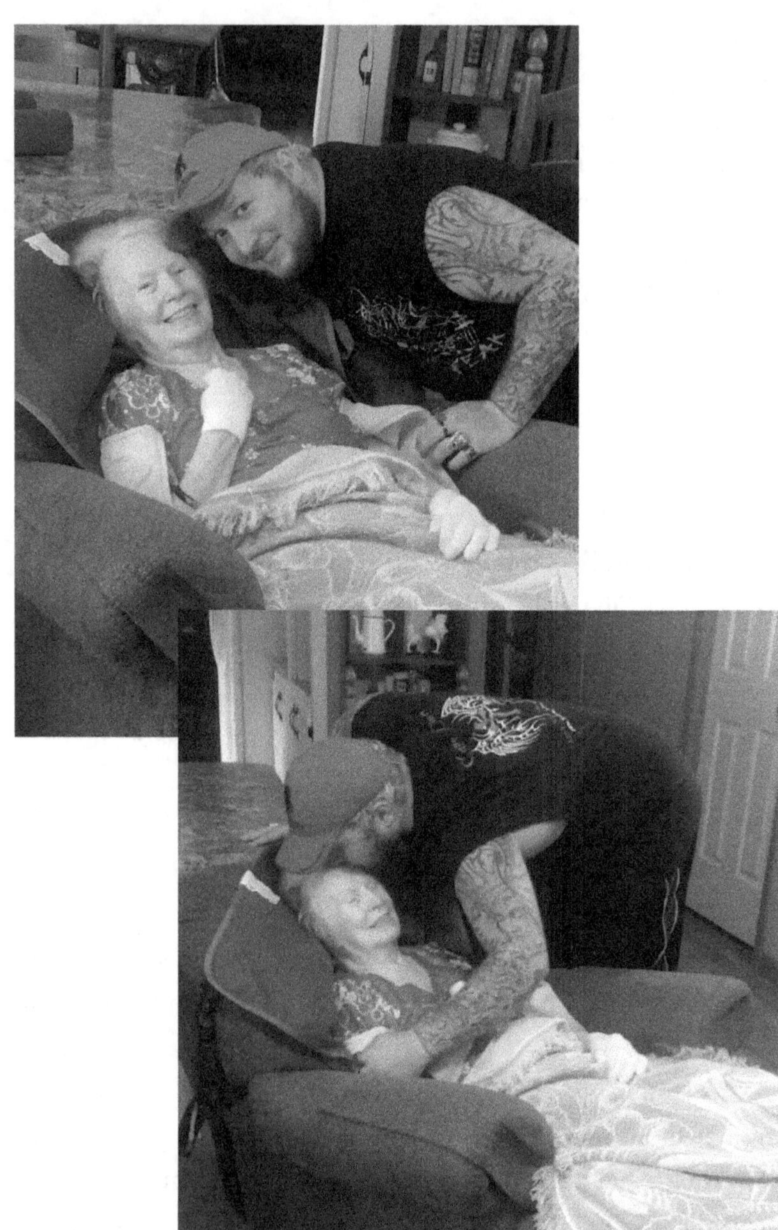

A picture of forgiveness. Seth praying for the woman who hit him.

bring peace and healing to us all that day. She passed away two weeks later.

When we crossed back over the bridge to come home, Seth showed me his phone again. He had added a word: FORGIVENESS.

What's living rent-free in your head? What's occupying space that could be filled with gratitude, joy, and happiness? Unforgiveness is an emotional parasite that sucks the life and beauty out of your being. Who do you need to release today? Maybe it's someone else. Perhaps it's yourself. Today is the day for you to walk in freedom.

Letting go will be the making of you, or unforgiveness will be the breaking of you.

If you are ready to take the next step, write a letter to the person you need to forgive. The written word is powerful. You can read it after you've written it to ensure your words don't come off with daggers but with grace. Write as many drafts as you need. You can tear it up, throw it away, burn it, or put a stamp on it and mail it. No matter what you decide, it's liberating to release it.

What do you replace that space with? Fill it with gratitude. Start by writing down five things you are grateful for. Will it be easy? No. Will it be worth it? Absolutely. This is a turning point, and only you have the power to decide which path you want for your future. Letting go will be the making of you, or unforgiveness will be the breaking of you. You're stronger than you know. Make the right choice.

Chapter 21

SETH TODAY

"I'm already loved, I'm already chosen
I know who I am, I know what You've spoken
I'm already loved, more than I can imagine
And that is enough...."

— Lyrics from *Jireh* by Elevation
Worship and Maverick City Music

As I put the finishing touches on these pages, Seth is recovering nicely from his eighteenth surgery! The irony of this most recent surgery, which happened on March 8, 2022, is that it took place at the same hospital where they had airlifted him in 2011. Not only that, but the following day they moved him to another floor of the ICU–the fifth floor, where he had been placed ten and a half years ago. Can you guess what room they put him in? Yep. The exact same room he was in after his initial surgery. All of these things were trauma triggers for me, as you can imagine. The sights, smells, and all-too-familiar landscape of that hospital floor and room threatened to undo me, but here's the deal: I knew I could get past the triggers. I've done it many times before, and I knew, without a doubt, that the Lord was with me yet again. Not only that, but he gave me the gift of my new husband, who stayed by my side. While Seth was in surgery, my man did what he does so well—he encouraged me amid these challenges.

Due to COVID-19 restrictions, we were not allowed to hang out at the hospital while waiting for the results of Seth's surgery. The waiting rooms were "closed." So, we had to wait, wonder, and pray outside the hospital. We mostly hung out in the parking lot, though we knew it could be a long wait. We were told the surgery would take anywhere from two to nine hours, an unnerving span of time. Always the overachiever, Seth ended up being in surgery for thirteen hours! It was a long, agonizing day. As his time in surgery continued for hours, it magnified my imagination. Worse case scenarios invaded my mind, and as it turned out, the surgery took as long as it did because what they discovered when they opened him up *was* a worst-case scenario. But God was in the details, and this "worst case" ended up being a blessing.

As the surgeons worked on Seth, they discovered that his accident with the 18-wheeler had done more damage than messing with his graft. There was more going on underneath the surface than doctors initially realized. A piece of bone had been fractured and fragmented. It was floating freely in his skull. No wonder Seth had been in so much pain. For months before this surgery, he was still leaking brain fluid and couldn't bend forward due to the pain he experienced with that movement. He started to suffer from seizures (and then he suffered from the medication to help with the seizures). He would say he felt like he was in a horror movie. His brain felt like it was on fire. Seth also told us he felt like someone was ripping his skull apart with a chainsaw. He could hear crunching sounds in his head! All this happened because a piece of a bone was free-floating in his skull and hitting his brain. It had sharp edges, so it was actually cutting into it! Thankfully, the bone fragment was found along with an infection during this latest surgery, and both were removed. Neither had shown up on his CT scans, so the neurosurgeon didn't know what was happening until the day of surgery. Doctors also took an 8cm x 8cm piece of his left Latissimus muscle and the main artery from that site to revise the graft on his head (yes, Grim Reaper is gone). They took two

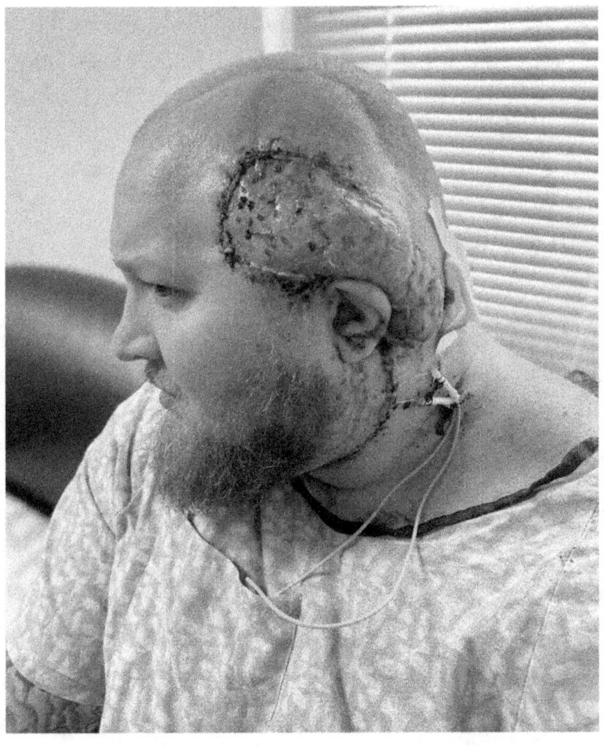

Seth's revised skin graft one week post-surgery

large skin grafts from his left thigh to cover the exposed muscle on his head.

As horrible as this has been for Seth, physically and emotionally, we are even more hopeful that he can move forward now that this surgery has remedied the issues he was experiencing. Those thirteen hours in the capable hands of the surgeons were a Godsend. As I write this and he is recovering, I can see (just a couple of weeks after surgery) that Seth is already processing better. He is also speaking more words! I believe this setback has launched his greatest comeback. He still experiences pain and has since September 28, 2011, but Seth carries on one day at a time. Today, he is alive and well– encouraging, inspiring, and of course, continuing to make people laugh with his TikTok videos!

Hopes, Dreams, Plans

You may be wondering what Seth's hopes, dreams, and plans for the future are at this point. He is asked that a lot. Since this last surgery, Seth says he's thinking even more deeply these days. He wants more than ever for those who don't know Christ to come to a saving knowledge of Him; to have a relationship with Jesus. As Seth knows, life is fragile and unpredictable, so he longs for people to accept Christ before they die so they can go to heaven and live eternally with Jesus. (This life is temporary for all of us, but heaven is for eternity.) Seth continues to put this longing into action. He is also beginning to set new goals for himself. At the time of writing this book, he still has not been fully released to train at a hundred percent, but he's getting stronger every day. He's looking forward to pursuing the Paralympics again, but he's not yet sure that's what God has for him. What is certain is that any goal he sets for himself, he will commit to it. (Hopefully, none of those goals will include pranking his mother!)

In earlier chapters, I've given some examples of Seth sharing his testimony and pointing others to the Lord. After undergoing his eighteenth surgery, I recently witnessed Seth ministering to the nurses as he lay in his ICU bed! I went into my usual bit with each nurse, saying, "Okay, take care of this guy because this is what happened to him...." I'd share enough about his story so they would know. Then Seth would chime in and ask each nurse how they were doing. He'd pray with them, flirt with them and make them laugh, and then tell them about God's love and His goodness. His gentleness and sincerity touched their hearts. Several commented, "You have no idea how God used you today. It's nothing compared to what you're going through, but I've been going through some hard things...." After surgery, as he lay in his hospital bed with four drains coming out of his head and IVs in his arm, he would smile through his pain and minister to whoever entered his room.

Seth knows this is his purpose: to love others and point them to Christ wherever he may be and in the midst of whatever he is going through. There is nothing more fulfilling for him—or me. Seth knows that he is in perfect alignment with his calling, and it shows. None of us are here to just suck oxygen. Like Nick Vujicic, an Australian man born without any arms or legs, Seth takes advantage of the opportunities God gives him to help others. Nick, a strong Christian and famous motivational speaker, said, "I'm officially disabled, but I'm truly enabled because of my lack of limbs. My unique challenges have opened up unique opportunities to reach so many in need."

Seth can say the same thing about the challenges he lives with as a result of his traumatic brain injury. God has given each of us an assignment, a purpose to fulfill, a reason for living. Of course, there is so much we can't do. None of us can change the state of the world, but we can have an impact where God has us at this moment. Every one of us, no matter our disabilities or limitations, has a sphere of influence. We all have a chance to give hope to someone that crosses our path during the day. An encouraging word can make all the difference. It may not seem like much at the time, but it's like planting a seed. Over time, it will take root and blossom. Trust the seed even if you don't see the results of your influence. God takes our efforts and blesses them. I've been on the giving and receiving end of this countless times, and I've had the pleasure of watching Seth use his influence to love others and point them to Jesus. It's a blessing to behold.

St. Francis of Assisi: "Start by doing what's necessary; then do what's possible; suddenly you are doing the impossible."

Every day I praise God that my son is still alive and kickin' and doing well, fulfilling his purpose in a way we would never have chosen. One day, like all of us who belong to Christ, he will get a new body, including a new brain, when God calls him to Heaven to live eternally with Him! Until then, Seth carries on in his earthly body, with all its limitations, and he does it with gusto. Though this book takes you only up to his 28th year of life, his life story is still very much being written. God is working out His plan for Seth, which gives him a future and ongoing hope.

Since you're reading this, you're alive, too, so your story is still being written! Like Seth, you are a survivor, and that's no small feat with all you've been through. Congratulations! (That goes for you too, caregivers.) Life is far from easy, but never give up. As you move forward in life, you would be wise to remember Psalm 121:2 (NIV) and take it to heart: *"My help comes from the Lord, the Maker of heaven and earth."* As strong as you are, you're not meant to do this alone. The Lover of Your Soul wants to help you. Knowing this has gotten Seth and me through the darkest of times and fueled us with hope. Will you embrace this truth? If you do, you won't regret it.

In Closing... Your Life, Your Choice

"For God has not given us a spirit of fear and timidity, but of power, and love, and self-discipline."

— 1 Timothy 1:7 (NLT)

I hope our story has been a help to you. I don't know the story surrounding your situation, but I'm sure you could write your own book with everything that has taken place in your life! No matter your circumstances, your *today* and your *future* are what you make of it. If you let the terrible things that happened to you define your life, you will quickly become disillusioned. The moment you begin to celebrate every blessing and every accomplishment, no matter how small, your perspective will shift. It is *your life* and *your choice* to see yourself as an overcomer. You're not just a survivor, but a thriver!

So, friend, get up, dust yourself off, and keep moving forward. Seth and I are cheering for you. Do something different today! Take your power back! Seize the day and seize your success. Take to heart the words of St. Francis of Assisi, "Start by doing what's necessary; then do what's possible; suddenly you are doing the impossible." Of course, by now, you know what this requires of you, even in your pain: ***Push Through It!***

Seth and Mom

If you would like to book us to speak at your next event, email us at TeamSethFoundation@gmail.com. The Team Seth Foundation For Traumatic Brain Injury Awareness is a 501c3 organization. Visit our website TeamSethFoundation.org to learn more about Seth's miracle.

Connect with us:

YouTube: youtube.com/@TeamSethFoundation

TikTok: tiktok.com/@teamsethfoundation

Instagram: instagram.com/teamsethfoundation

Pinterest: pin.it/5GCxsCW

Facebook: facebook.com/TeamSethFoundationTBI

ACKNOWLEDGMENTS

To my sisters, Tanya Renea and Melody Sullivan. Thank you for making the one-hour drive to New Orleans Children's Hospital to hold me up emotionally so I could continue to hold up my son. You two are my best friends and the shoulders I leaned on. It took both of you to hold me up because I was a mess. Tanya, thank you for not letting me waste away on hospital food. I am especially grateful for all the home-cooked meals you smuggled in.

To my mom, Gwen Cloud, thank you for being such a strong support and prayer warrior. You constantly assured me, from the beginning, that God was going to bring our boy through this. Thank you for being there every single day when Seth came home and helping with everything, from house cleaning to laundry, to encouraging me.

To the three of you, thank you for listening to me vent my hurt, frustration, and anger without judgment. The weekly conference calls I made during my five-hour drive back home were the therapy that allowed me to exhale so I could be strong for Seth emotionally.

To our amazing Team Seth Family, we love you and appreciate you all so much. The prayers and encouraging messages telling us how Seth's story has positively impacted your life were the reminders we need to keep pushing through.

Thank you to the medical staff and therapists who have touched our lives throughout this journey. Our paths may have crossed due to Seth's medical needs, but you never failed to show genuine care and concern. It made the countless doctor visits and surgeries easier, knowing your heart was in it.

Thank you to my Publishing Team: Alisa Vielman, Angela Aja, and Cathy McIlvoy. It took a village to bring this story to light, and you three girls are mine.

Alisa, I am convinced you are a cyborg of some sort. You are such a blessing to me and Seth. You helped me to push through the emotional days I didn't think I could bear to climb back into the dreaded time machine. Thank you for always being the on-call encourager when I felt it was too difficult to relive the painful journey. You have been there on my darkest days. You are truly a blessing.

Angela, you are a great author's coach. Thank you for putting the pen in my hand and reminding me that someone is crying themselves to sleep tonight because they need the hope found in my story. You kept me on track, giving me that gentle nudge (or more of a shove) out of the shallows of comfortability. Ships were meant to sail in deep waters, not stayed tied to the shore.

Cathy, thank you for helping pull out more details of my story. You helped me convey my words beautifully.

Finally, thank you to our Lord and Savior, Jesus Christ. This is your story. We are simply the characters you entrusted to live it for the world to see. There are some things we experience that we don't understand, and you are good enough to allow us to ask, "Why." It's obvious your hand is at work in this. Only you can take what was meant for our demise and turn it around for our good...you truly bring beauty from ashes.

To all who mourn in Israel, he will give a crown of beauty for ashes, a joyous blessing instead of mourning....

— Isaiah 61:3 NLT

ABOUT THE AUTHOR

Kimber Hanchey-Ogden is the senior pastor at Redemption Power Church. She is an author, life coach, and motivational speaker with 34 years of experience serving in ministry.

She founded The Team Seth Foundation For Traumatic Brain Injury Awareness, a 501c3 organization that assists children diagnosed with brain injury. A public speaker and advocate, Kimber has lobbied before the state legislature for funds, assistance, and equal opportunities for children with disabilities. Active in her community, she served as Special Olympics Director for Northeast and North Central Louisiana for several years.

Kimber is passionate about empowering people with purpose and equipping them to lead. She is a keynote conference speaker qualified to speak on topics such as Biblical passages, leadership, marriage and relationships, and mental health.

If you would like to book Kimber to speak at your next event or to schedule a life coaching session, email her at KimberHancheyOgden@gmail.com.